HUSBAND
& WIFE

HUSBAND & WIFE

The sexes in Scripture and society

Peter DeJong
Donald R. Wilson

ZONDERVAN
PUBLISHING HOUSE OF THE ZONDERVAN CORPORATION
GRAND RAPIDS, MICHIGAN 49506

HUSBAND & WIFE: THE SEXES IN SCRIPTURE AND SOCIETY
COPYRIGHT © 1979 by Peter DeJong and Donald R. Wilson

Library of Congress Cataloging in Publication Data

DeJong, Peter, 1945-
   Husband & wife.

   Includes bibliographical references.
   1. Sex (Theology) 2. Marriage. 3. Sex role. I. Wilson, Donald Reid,
1931-   joint author. II. Title.
BT708.D44   261.8'34'1   78-11989
ISBN 0-310-37760-9

Printed in the United States of America

All Scripture quotations are from the New International Version. Used by permission. Copyright ©1973, 1978 by New York International Bible Society.

To Char, my wife, with love and respect. Her insight and support as a partner in Christ prompted much of what is set down here.

CONTENTS

PREFACE

Over the past decade, the topic of male and female roles in American society has come to be of great interest to both scholars and the general public. This has led to the publication of a great number of books in three categories:

(1) anthologies of writings about the social position of today's woman by members of the "women's liberation movement," (2) analyses of the changing roles of women and men by social scientists, and (3) discussions of the biblical evidence bearing on the male-female relationship. Each type presents only part of what evangelical Christians need to know in order to respond wisely to the changes that are taking place in sex roles.

In this book we will examine three types of evidence: biological, social-scientific, and biblical. By integrating these three types, we will attempt to construct a Christian perspective on the changing roles of women and men.

My professional role is that of a sociology teacher in a Christian liberal arts college. Teaching in this context demands that the Christian social scientist consistently integrate faith and scholarship. Most publications that have treated the relation of social science to the Christian faith have done so at a fairly abstract philosophical level. Professor Wilson and I are convinced, however, that the concepts and empirical data of social science, when properly understood and carefully applied, can offer much concrete help to the Christian community as it responds to the social issues of the day.

This book is a tangible expression of that belief. It should be of value in the courses on marriage and the family taught at Christian liberal arts college, as well as in classes that deal specifically with the changing roles of the sexes. And I hope it will be of use to many others who in one capacity or another are pondering the complementary roles of Christian husbands and wives.

No small book could deal fully with all the implications of the vast array of evidence bearing on contemporary sex roles. The discussion questions that follow each chapter of this book are meant to encourage the reader to apply the positions developed in the chapter to his or her own circumstances. Also, each chapter offers suggestions for additional reading.

Professor Donald Wilson is responsible for a significant share of this book. The sections on the male-female relationship in Creation, the Fall, and redemption that constitute most of chapter 6 are his work. They show him to be, I believe, a very fine and sensitive scholar.

There are others whose help I would like to acknowledge: Warren Boer, for encouraging me to take on this project; Ruth Rinsema and Kris Vande Lune, for doing research for me and for proofreading earlier versions of the manuscript; Nell Faber, for typing the manuscript; my colleagues in the sociology department, for stimulating my thinking and for freeing the time I needed to write; and Paul Hillman, Zondervan's textbook editor, for giving me the benefit of his editorial skills and for encouraging the publication of this book. Finally, the love and encouragement of Char DeJong must not go unrecognized.

PETER DEJONG

/1/

SOCIAL CHANGE AFFECTING THE TRA- DITIONAL FEMALE AND MALE ROLES

When God created human beings, He created two biolog- ically distinct types: males and females. The first ques- tion likely to be asked about a newborn child in any soci- ety is: "Is it a boy or a girl?" The answer has profound implications for the whole of the child's life, because every society expects women and men to be "different."

The expected differences are not limited to physical characteristics. Each society also expects females and males to accomplish different tasks, to play different roles in society. This division of tasks between males and females can be considered to center on the family. The establishment of "women's work" and "men's work" serves to organize both the day-to-day activities of family members and the relation of the family as a whole to the larger society. In this respect roles in American society do not differ from those in other societies.

The traditional adult female role is that of mother and housewife. As a mother, the female not only bears the children but also has the major share of the task in rearing them. She must instill in them the values the family considers important, concern herself with their emotional needs, and handle their daily physical needs.

The concept of housewife involves two sets of obligations: caring for the household and being a wife. Care of the household includes such duties as buying food and preparing the family's meals, buying and maintaining clothing, decorating the house, arranging for the repair of malfunctioning items around the house, and chauffeuring the children—and perhaps her husband at times— to their various activities.

As the traditional wife, the woman is expected to be affectionate toward her husband and sexually accessible to him. She should loyally subordinate her own interests to his occupational interests "for the economic good of the whole family." This may mean, in part, that she is on call to entertain the husband's business associates at the home and is willing to settle where job opportunities are most appealing to him. She is expected to contribute information and her own opinions to the decision-making process in the family, but she must also realize that the final authority resides with her husband. Finally, the traditional wife is expected to accept a dependent social and economic status. Her status depends upon her husband's position in the community and his economic activities.

The traditional adult male role is that of provider and husband. As a provider, the male must earn a living for his family. This generally means finding a job, doing well in it, and making provision for the family's economic security in the event of his death.

His obligations as a husband include being affectionate toward his wife and sexually accessible to her. The traditional husband is also the acknowledged head of the family. As such he is expected to represent the family in the larger community and to provide the final authority in matters of discipline and in decisions that affect the family as a whole.[1]

In summary, the traditional female role is geared toward making a home. The adult woman fulfills it by being a nurturant mother to her children, an efficient housekeeper for the family, and a loving, helpful, and obedient wife to her husband. The traditional female role focuses on the internal day-to-day activities of the family. The traditional male role, on the other hand, is geared toward supporting the home. The adult male fulfills it by being a faithful provider and benevolent decision maker for the family. The traditional male role focuses on the relation of the family as a whole to the larger society.

These are the dominant cultural ideals for males and females in American society. Of course, the way in which these ideals are expressed may vary somewhat among different economic, religious, and ethnic groups. For instance, the fact that lower-class women held jobs long before it was culturally acceptable to do so was a reflection of their economic circumstances, not of a different ideal for the female role.

The Changes

The Industrial Revolution triggered a series of technological and associated social changes that altered the American family and the character of tasks assigned to women and men. Although these changes, which resulted in the shift from an agricultural to a modern industrial society, have been going on for more than two hundred years, they did not affect male and female roles significantly until the last century. Less than a hundred years ago American society was primarily rural and agricultural. In 1850, even though America was urbanizing and industrializing, over four-fifths of the population still lived in rural areas and about two-thirds of the labor force was engaged in farming.[2] In this agricultural economy, the sexes were acting out their roles in the full traditional sense.

Technological and social change has accelerated tremendously during the last century, causing notable alterations in sex roles, particularly for the female. American women have been freed from many of the tasks traditionally associated with the housewife-mother role, or at least have been enabled to spend less time doing them.

In the agricultural society of the past, women performed many tasks that have since been removed from the home.[3] A man who took a wife a century ago expected not only a companion but also a business associate. Women had the productive tasks of baking bread, churning butter, canning fruits and vegetables, making clothes, making soap, and even concocting medicines. Through industrialization these tasks were gradually transferred from the home to specialized economic agencies. American society now has bakeries, food-processing plants, clothing manufacturers, soap factories, and pharmaceutical firms. With the removal of these tasks from the home, women's apparent economic contribution to society diminished, and in time the phrase "just a housewife" appeared.

Today some women allot as much time to housekeeping as their mothers did, but they need not do so to gain the same results. The development of gas and electricity has made the storing and preparing of food more efficient. Washing machines, dryers, vacuum cleaners, steam irons, and other mechanical devices have simplified other household tasks. Now that less time is required to keep house, women can, if they wish, devote more time to other pursuits.[4]

The obligations in the role of mother have also been reduced.[5] A century and a half ago, most of the child's education took place in the home. Although there was some teaching of the "three R's" in schools, formal schooling did not take up a significant share of most people's lives. The past century has witnessed both a great expansion of formal education and the transfer of many types of education from the home to the school. Practically all children are required to attend school by the age of five or six, and some start nursery school as early as three. Salaried educators increasingly teach everything from how to button coats and tie shoes to how to run a government. Schooling not only starts at an earlier age but also takes up more of the child's day and continues for more years. A full high school education is now the rule, and college and graduate education are common.

Besides removing or reducing many tasks, technological change has also affected the female role by making effective and convenient methods of contraception widely available. *Coitus interruptus*, sexual abstinence, and even the condom have been in use as contraceptive methods for centuries, but the more desirable and effective methods did not become generally available until well into the nineteenth century. By the mid-1800s, efficient manufacturing procedures and the invention of vulcanized rubber finally made it feasible to mass-produce the condom and the vaginal diaphragm.[6]

Significant change regarding contraception has occurred in the twentieth century. A burgeoning world population, an active birth-control movement, and changing views about ideal family size have made America a contracepting society. Over 90 percent of its married couples have used or intend to use some form of contraception, and when we add to this figure the 5 percent who know they are sterile, it is obvious that very few Americans are now willing to let children come unplanned.[7] Couples are using contraception earlier in their marriages, and groups that used to be uninformed about birth control or disinclined to adopt it—Catholics, the less educated, the poor, and racial minorities—have shown large gains in contraceptive use over the past two decades.

Modern contraceptive techniques have given women much more control over their reproductive capacity, and this control, coupled with changing attitudes about the ideal number of children in our materialistic, consumption-oriented society, has led to a notable reduction in family size. It is estimated that women who passed through the childbearing years a century ago had an average of 5.0 children. This figure fell to 2.6 in the two decades following World War II.[8] And if the birth rate of the mid-seventies continues, the average number of children per family will drop below 2.0.

Not only are women having fewer children today, but they are marrying earlier, completing their childbearing sooner, and, with the help of modern medicine, living longer.[9] The average American wife and mother marries at the age of twenty, has her first child two years later, and completes her childbearing before she is thirty. She is likely to see her children marry while she is still in her forties. This leaves her with the "empty nest" for twenty-five to thirty years, since seventy-five is her life expectancy.

The situation of the American woman, then, is very different than it was a century ago. Traditional housewife-mother tasks have been passed from the home to specialized agencies in the larger society, or at least have been reduced through the development of labor-saving devices. Furthermore, technological developments in contraception and health care have allowed women to have fewer children and a longer life. This means that the modern woman potentially has a great deal more time free for nonhousewife activities.

The Effects on Traditional
Sex Roles

Earlier in this century, as society came to recognize the impact of societal changes that reduced the amount of time required by traditional female tasks, the question became: "What should the respectable woman do with her extra time?" Society responded by informally encouraging women to engage in what sociologist Talcott Parsons has called the "common humanistic pattern."[10]

This pattern consists of two sets of activities. The first is developing artistic interests and educated tastes. Women were encouraged to spend part of their time in the "cultural affairs" of the community. They were to help organize and maintain local music and drama groups, museums, and art galleries. They also were expected to develop their own abilities in these areas and to use these abilities in their homes. A creatively and tastefully decorated home gave a woman status.

The other aspect of the "common humanistic pattern" focused on community welfare. Women were to collect money for the fight against polio, cancer, heart disease, and other ills. They were expected to volunteer time to community agencies in such roles as tutors, clothing and furniture collectors, and foster parents. They might also participate in church-based groups meant to supplement the social-welfare activities of community agencies.

In this way, society extended traditional female tasks outside the home. The activities that are a part of caring for the home were now to be exercised toward the whole community. It was a neat extension because the requirements remained the same. To be successful at both types of "care," women should be oriented toward nurturing and serving.

Earlier in this century, this humanistic pattern was the only culturally sanctioned addition to the traditional female responsibilities of housewife and mother. Many American women who had the time available accepted this culturally prescribed role addition, and its practice has continued. Since 1940, however, women have stepped up their participation in yet another role—that of paid worker.

Woman's entry into the role of paid worker (and hence provider) has not been easy. It has been denounced by church leaders, politicians, community leaders, nonworking women, and psychiatrists. Even many working women themselves (the term "working women"—i.e., employed women—is not meant to suggest that nonemployed women do not work) have been ambivalent about it. Many have felt guilty about an activity that is perceived to compete at times with the responsibilities of child and household care. Yet despite the criticism and ambivalence, statistics show a fairly consistent trend upward in the rate of female employment.

Table 1.1 shows the extent to which women have participated in the labor force over the past eighty-five years. (Before 1890, reliable data were not collected by the U.S. Bureau of the Census.) It reveals that relatively little change occurred between 1890 and 1930. In 1890, 18 percent of work-age women were employed; by 1930 this figure had risen only to 24 percent.[11]

The greatest increase occurred in the years right after 1940. In 1940, 29 percent of the female population sixteen and older was in the labor force. Then many men went off to war, and a considerable demand for female labor power developed. In the next five years, 5.5 million women were added to the labor force; 38 percent of adult women were employed in 1945.

When World War II ended, men returned to their civilian jobs, and society made it clear again that woman's place was in the home. By 1947 the rate of female participation in the labor force had dropped to 31 percent. Since

1.1/WOMEN IN THE CIVILIAN LABOR FORCE, SELECTED YEARS, 1890-1975

Year	Number (in thousands)	As Percentage of Total Labor Force	As Percentage of Adult Female Population
1890	3,704	17	18
1900	4,999	18	20
1920	8,229	20	23
1930	10,396	22	24
1940	13,783	25	29
1945	19,290	36	38
1947	16,664	28	31
1950	18,389	30	34
1955	20,548	32	36
1960	23,240	33	38
1965	26,200	35	39
1970	31,520	38	43
1975	36,998	40	46

SOURCE: Francine D. Blau, "Women in the Labor Force: An Overview," in *Women: A Feminist Perspective*, ed. Jo Freeman (Palo Alto, Calif.: Mayfield Publishing Co., 1975), p. 217. Figures for 1975 are from U.S. Bureau of the Census, **Statistical Abstract of the United States: 1976** (Washington, D.C.: U.S. Government Printing Office, 1976), p. 356. As Blau states, pre-1940 figures in this table include women fourteen and older, while figures for 1940 and after include women sixteen and older. This is due to a procedural change by the Bureau of the Census.

then, however, women have steadily returned to the labor force. By the mid-fifties the number of women workers had surpassed its wartime high, and participation rates regained their 1945 levels in the early sixties. By 1975, 46 percent of adult women were gainfully employed; they made up fully 40 percent of the civilian labor force. This level of participation is the highest ever.

Perhaps even more striking are the changes in the types of women taking paid jobs. Owing in part to the traditional belief that the mother who worked for pay would damage her children as well as upset the functioning of her home, the typical pre-1940 female worker was either young and single or widowed or divorced. Since 1950, however, more and more married women with children have been entering the labor force.

Table 1.2 shows that there has been relatively little change in employment rates for single women and widowed or divorced women. In 1940, 48 percent of single women were gainfully employed; by 1975 the figure had risen only to 57 percent. The rate for widowed or divorced women increased only 6 percent, from 32 to 38 percent. Society generally has considered it appropriate for a woman to assume the role of provider if she does not have a husband.

The dramatic change has been in the employment rate of married women who are living with their husbands. From 1940 to 1975 that rate almost tripled, from 15 to 44 percent. And among married women with children ages six through seventeen, the employment rate has more than quintupled, from an estimated 9 percent in 1940 to 52 percent in 1975. Among mothers with children under six, the 1950 figure was 13 percent; by 1975 it had grown to 37 percent.

The figures make it clear that a large proportion of American women are simultaneously playing the traditional housewife-mother role and the provider role of

1.2/TYPES OF WOMEN IN THE LABOR FORCE, 1940-1975

Marital Status	Percent in Labor Force				
	1940	1950	1960	1970	1975
Single	48	51	44	53	57
Widowed, or Divorced	32	36	37	36	38
Married, living with husband	15	24	31	41	44
(No children under 18)	(a)	(30)	(35)	(42)	(44)
(Children 6-17 years only)	9(b)	(28)	(39)	(49)	(52)
(Children 0-5 years old)	(a)	(13)	(19)	(31)	(37)

SOURCE: U.S. Bureau of the Census, **Statistical Abstract: 1976**, pp. 358-59.
(a) No information available.
(b) Estimated in F. Ivan Nye and Felix M. Berardo, **The Family: Its Structure and Interaction**
(New York: The Macmillan Co., 1973), p. 271.

paid worker, a combination that society used to consider unacceptable. This has brought about a number of changes in American family life. Research shows that employed wives tend to have more decision-making authority in the family than nonemployed wives; that is, their families tend to be less patriarchal and more egalitarian.[12] Employed mothers share more household tasks with husbands and children than their nonemployed counterparts.[13] And there has been an increased transfer of early child-rearing responsibilities from the family to day-care centers and nurseries.

Long-range technological and social changes have also affected the traditional male role, though to a lesser extent. The central task of the adult male role is still that of providing for the family. However, the place where he does this has changed. A century and a half ago, most men were farmers. They did their work near their homes with the assistance of their wives and children. Today most employed men leave home early in the morning and return late in the afternoon. This means that their opportunities to supervise their children and teach them values have diminished. In addition, farm fathers could teach their children occupational skills. Today most job training must be passed on to trained instructors in a formal school system.

Male and female roles are reciprocal and complementary, and so as the female role changes, the male role changes also. As more married women work, more men find themselves sharing the decision-making authority in the home with their wives and also taking on some household tasks once thought to belong exclusively to women.

Some have heralded these changes in the female and male roles as a fundamental transformation in sex-role behavior and family life. Yet the changes, significant though they are, have certainly not advanced to the point where society expects men and women to share equally the responsibilities of providing for the family, making family decisions, rearing children, and caring for the home. Rather, the sexes support each other in these activities more than in the past. What has occurred, then, is not a fundamental change but a partial blurring of sex roles.

The Contemporary Feminist
Movement: Accentuating
Sex-Role Change

Today's feminist movement is devoted to changing the traditional definitions of women and men in society. The movement developed only in the late sixties, and so it cannot take credit for the partial blurring of sex roles that was well under way by that time. Yet it has done much to identify the pertinent issues, and it may thus serve to accelerate role change.

The current feminist movement can be traced to a number of events in our recent history. If a society espouses equality of opportunity but withholds it from a certain group of people, that society is ripe for a social movement directed at wiping out the inequity. However, the social movement will not get off the ground unless amorphous feelings of injustice are transformed into articulate statements about inequitable conditions and how they can be changed. The publication of landmark works like Simone de Beauvoir's *The Second Sex* and Betty Friedan's *The Feminine Mystique* served this function for the women's movement. These books, along with many others, did a great deal to articulate dissatisfaction with the traditional role of women and stimulate thought and action about women's position in society.

In a rather ironic way, the origin of the contemporary women's movement is linked to the radical element of the black civil-rights movement and the radical student movement of the sixties. Initially, the "New Left" of the sixties was male dominated and very insensitive to the issue of women's rights. The first position paper on women in the New Left was written in 1964 by Ruby Doris Smith Robinson, one of the founders of the SNCC (Student Non-Violent Coordinating Committee, a radical black civil-rights organization).[14] Little attention was paid to the paper; most of the attention it did receive took the form of mockery. In the same year Stokely Carmichael, also of the SNCC, made his inflammatory comment that "the only position for women in the SNCC is prone." In 1966, at an SDS (Students for a Democratic Society) convention, women demanded that female liberation be dealt with in the form of a resolution. They were again ridiculed.

So the female members of the New Left, a movement dedicated to the overthrow of a racist, exploitative social order, found that the radical vision did not extend to their own position in society. As a result, many of these women formed their own organizations specifically directed toward rooting out sexism.

In the broader historical perspective, the rise of the current feminist movement can be tied to the labor-force activity of women during and after World War II. As discussed earlier, women entered the labor force in great numbers as men were called away to fight. The federal government responded quickly by passing the Lanham Act, which allocated federal funds for the establishment of day-care centers.[15] Training programs were set up to teach newly employed female workers the skills they needed to do work formerly thought inappropriate for them. For the duration of the war, women were not only permitted but encouraged to assume positions of authority and responsibility previously unavailable to them.

Conditions changed after the war. When men returned to the labor force, women were again told their place was in the home. Federal financing for day-care centers dried up, and the training programs for women ceased. Women's participation in the labor force dwindled temporarily.

Many women, however, chose not to leave the role of paid employee, and in time it became evident that the employed mother might well become a permanent fixture of family life. Society's response was to attribute a number of serious social and personal problems to the mother's new role as paid worker.[16] The competing demands of her dual role were thought to account for increases in juvenile delinquency and to impair children's emotional development. Many people, professionals included, argued that a wife's encroaching on the husband's role as provider created a psychological threat to the husband's ego and hence a source of family instability.

Besides confronting a negative societal response to their entrance into the labor force, employed women found themselves channeled into certain types of jobs and discriminated against in other ways. There is a great deal of sexual segregation in the labor force. Half of all working women are employed in just 21 of the 250 occupations listed by the U.S. Bureau of the Census.[17] Just five occupations—secretary, household worker, bookkeeper, elementary school teacher, and waitress—account for one-fourth of all employed women. Not only were females channeled into "women's jobs" but they also found themselves being paid less than men, often for the same duties.[18] And women, like members of racial minorities, were passed over for job promotions in favor of similarly qualified white males.

The activity of women in the labor force during and after World War II, then, provided much of the impetus for the current feminist movement. By responding negatively to married women's increased employment, society reaffirmed that the housewife-mother role remained normative. This, coupled with occupational channeling and other forms of discrimination against women in the labor force, provided a set of concrete issues that writers like Friedan could focus on. These writers played a major role in initiating the present women's movement.

The various feminist organizations in the United States can be cataloged according to the conventional political categories of "radical" (i.e., holding that the status quo is repulsive and that a completely new social order is needed) and "reformist" (holding that society is basically sound but needs many improvements). If either of these categories of feminist organizations succeeded in achieving its goals, there would be a significant reorganization of sex roles and family life in American society.[19]

Most radical feminist organizations are independent groups scattered around the country. Usually they have no official name, preferring such designations as "the Tuesday night group." A few have adopted more colorful names: the Radical Feminists, Redstockings, SCUM (Society for Cutting Up Men), and WITCH (Women's International Terrorist Conspiracy from Hell). These radical groups initially captured the attention of the mass media with such unconventional activities as standing on street corners whistling at men, burning bras, and demonstrating against beauty pageants. They are also different from other feminist organizations in that they lack a nationwide organization. They reject structure and hierarchical leadership and emphasize the idea of "everyone doing her own thing." The various groups are linked only by writings and by word of mouth. The result of this lack of organization has been in the words of one observer, "political impotence."[20]

The women's liberation group of this sort is composed of about ten to fifteen members who come together in "consciousness-raising" or "rap" groups. Here they try to understand their own lives and dissatisfactions in terms of the social pressures that affect all women. The primary goal of the group is not personal therapy for the participants but rather a critical analysis of American society as it relates to women. Generally it is agreed that the institutions of American society are male dominated and that this domination accounts for "the oppression of women." Group members are critical of family, religious, legal, governmental, and economic institutions, all of which they perceive to play a part in relegating women to second-class citizenship.

The reformist organizations seek to expand women's rights within existing society. The most prominent among them is the National Organization for Women (NOW), established in 1966 by Betty Friedan and others. NOW is the only large national organization in the women's movement; in the mid-seventies it claimed a membership of some 40,000. It is a hierarchical organization of women and men with both a national structure and local groups.

NOW accepts the basic structure of American society in

many respects but feels society is badly in need of reform. It seeks to improve the status of women by holding conventions, hiring lobbyists, pursuing court cases on discrimination against women, holding orderly demonstrations, and publishing literature on the legal and economic status of women. NOW's major concerns have been to end discrimination against women in obtaining jobs and in pay, to secure pro-abortion laws, to equalize educational opportunity, and to procure state-supported child-care facilities. More recently its members have been working for legislation that would better protect women from wife-battering, rape, and pornographic violence.

Because of their organization and their less threatening reformist mode of operation, NOW and similar groups have been more successful in bringing about social change than the more radical elements in the movement. Political scientist Jo Freeman reports that under pressure from women's rights groups, the Equal Employment Opportunity Commission has been forced to take the issue of discrimination against women more seriously.[21] The result has been more rulings in favor of women. NOW and its sister organizations continue to file suits under the sex provision of Title VII of the 1964 Civil Rights Act. In 1972, Congress passed the proposed Equal Rights Amendment to the Constitution, which provides that "equality of rights under the law shall not be denied or abridged by the United States or by any State on account of sex." The Supreme Court has decriminalized abortion. Complaints of discrimination have been filed against hundreds of colleges and universities and many businesses. NOW and its sister organizations have played a major role in all these developments.

The contemporary feminist movement, then, did not initiate the partial blurring of traditional sex roles in American society. However, it is fast becoming a significant social force that contributes to this blurring process.

*Sex-Role Change: Issues
for Christians*

In the past, American Christians generally accepted the traditional division of labor between the sexes. The idea that women and men should engage in different tasks was thought to be consistent with the belief that God created males and females as biologically distinct. If questioned about the reasons for sex roles, the average Christian responded with a mixture of biblically related and culturally conditioned beliefs about the inherent natures of the two sexes. The organization of society by traditional sex roles was not a troublesome issue.

Now Christians are faced with some questions they haven't had to confront before. Should mothers be encouraged to stay home rather than get jobs? Does the release of young children to day-care centers and nurseries hinder their emotional development? Is a single maternal figure necessary for the stable personality development of children? Do the children of working mothers perform as well in school as the children of nonworking mothers? Are they more likely to become delinquent? How is the husband of a working woman affected? Is he psychologically threatened when his wife takes over a share of the provider role? Is the wife's employment a source of conflict in the husband-wife relationship? In general, are the families with working wives and mothers less stable? And what of the effects on the woman herself? Does the fact that she has to combine the paid-worker role with her more traditional female role put a strain on her? If so, what is the result for her physical and psychological health?

The organizational shifts in the family that accompany the blurring of sex roles also raise questions for Christians. Is it appropriate for the working wife to pass on some of her traditional responsibilities to the rest of the family? What are the implications of the fact that men now spend a large share of the day away from the home and hence may well be having less influence on their wives and children? Can Christians applaud the shift from a patriarchal to a more democratic authority structure in the family as more married women take on paid employment?

Finally, how should Christians respond to the many issues that the women's movement has forced society to take seriously? Should they support an Equal Rights Amendment if it not only would combat various forms of discrimination against women but also might extend alimony rights to men and compulsory military duty (if this is revived) to women? Should Christians support the position that the government should provide day care of children just as it provides public transportation and libraries? In general, should Christians support those forces in society working for full equality of opportunity between women and men.

Some Christians dismiss such questions. They insist that God created women and men with different natures and capabilities and that it is therefore perfectly logical for them to work at different tasks in society. God created woman to bear and rear children. He created man to be the head of the family and provide for it. To support their view, these Christians may point out that marriages recorded in Scripture fit this pattern.

Increasingly, however, a large portion of the Christian community is demanding more in-depth treatments of the biblical issues. Religious periodicals are devoting considerable space to biblically based articles about the functions and status of women in modern society. Books are appearing—two examples are Letha Scanzoni and Nancy Hardesty's *All We're Meant to Be* and James Olthuis's *I Pledge You My Troth*—that examine the biblical teachings on women, marriage, and the family.

Although the interpretations and conclusions vary, one

thing is evident throughout these treatments. The isolated interpretation and application of some passages in the Bible that deal with men and women leads to exegetical difficulties and generally results in confusion. Selecting Abraham and Sarah as complete ideals for contemporary Christian marriage partners is inadequate, since the Apostle Paul praised the very different marriage of Aquila and Priscilla. To interpret male headship (Eph. 5:22-23) as meaning that the husband should be the unilateral decision maker in the family seems to conflict with the previous verse, in which Paul instructs all Christians to be in subjection to one another. Basing one's position on carefully selected examples and culturally tinged interpretations of isolated texts is simplistic and can only distort God's revelation for men and women.

Theologians have long recognized the dangers of wooden literalism in biblical interpretation. As G. C. Berkouwer points out: "We have received the Word of God in human words, Greek, Hebrew, and Aramaic words. These words demand study and translation."[22] Christians must not force upon the Bible their own culturally conditioned understanding of certain words and ideas. Moreover, not every incident recorded in Scripture portrays a timeless doctrinal truth. Christians must interpret specific incidents in terms of the biblical norms behind the incidents, norms that reappear throughout the Bible. And these norms or fundamental truths must be responsibly applied so that Christians can try to live in accordance with God's revealed directives.

The Bible indicates that women and men are biologically distinct, but it does not go into detail about all the distinctions and how they affect the relative abilities of the sexes to accomplish different tasks. For instance, Scripture does not definitively teach that women are wholly responsible for the rearing of children. Rather, the command is that parents bring up children according to the norms of God (Prov. 22:6; Deut. 6:7). Children are commanded to obey both fathers and mothers (Exod. 20:12; Eph. 6:1-4), which suggests that both parents should play a part in child rearing. Similarly, Paul implies that both parents are to provide for their children (2 Cor. 12:14).

The Bible gives fundamental principles regarding the sexes and their behavior, not a full list of specific, timeless role obligations for each. And so, as with many other matters, the Christian community must take the basic principles revealed in the Bible and attempt to apply them to life in a complex, changing society.

The scholarship of the academic community can be of great help in this undertaking. As Scanzoni and Hardesty have said: "If all truth is God's truth, the insights from philosophy, the physical sciences, and the behavioral sciences may help us understand the biblical message."[23] Since in this book we want to bring both scientific evidence (especially in the area of sociology) and Christian teaching to bear on the modern sex-role issue, a look at the relationship between the two is needed.

On the Relation of Christianity and Sociology

For centuries the Christian community has had to grapple with the relation between science and the teachings of the Bible. Long and involved treatises have been written about how the assumptions and findings of the scientific method of understanding physical and biological reality are related to the nature of physical and biological reality as revealed in the Scriptures. These writings have by no means fully resolved the general issue. They have served, however, to defuse many specific issues, and they have brought about a general recognition that the natural sciences can help us understand God's created reality. For example, most Christians now readily acknowledge the value of biological knowledge that can be used to reduce suffering and lengthen life. Indeed, many Christians are interpreting the pursuit of this type of scientific understanding as a partial fulfillment of God's mandate to human beings to subdue the earth (Gen. 1:28).

The social or behavioral sciences hold a somewhat different position in the Christian community. They are more suspect than the natural sciences. One reason is that their theories sometimes contain assumptions (i.e., untested premises) that are at odds with the biblical account of the basic nature of men and women—that they are creatures created in the image of God (Gen. 1:26-27) who are responsible for their actions (Gen. 3:8-19). Christians often point to the "extreme behavioralism" of social scientists like B. F. Skinner, charging that such a perspective reduces human beings to automatons who are not responsible for their actions because they have been so thoroughly conditioned by their social experiences.

Christians who attack such perspectives do so rightly. However, it is wrong to identify *all* social-scientific theories with the "extreme behavioralist" outlook. Most social scientists admit that human beings are to one degree or another motivated by innate biological drives.[24] Some emphasize that human beings are self-interested. Although not couched in biblical terms, these theories often mirror what the Bible teaches about the nature of human beings, and consequently Christians can gain insights about God's created reality from them. In other words, social science can uncover aspects of God's created pattern in general revelation.

Admittedly, the main theme running through most social-scientific explanations (especially in sociology) is that human behavior is in large part formed by social influences, that is, the influences that human beings have on one another. However, for Christians to dismiss sociology or other social sciences because they feel this emphasis minimizes people's responsibility for their actions—or because it conflicts with the American cultural motif of individualism—is a grave error. God created human beings as social beings; people were meant to live with one another (Gen. 2:18-25). Repeatedly throughout Scripture there are teachings about the influence that human beings have on one another. For example, Christians are commanded to bring up their children in the way that they should go. The Christian community is to try to influence delinquent members back into its fellowship. The Great Commission instructs believers to go out and influence unbelievers so that they too may come to know Christ. Certainly it is the work of the Holy Spirit that brings unbelievers to Christ, but to say this is not to deny the reality of social influence.

Christians who minimize the importance of social influence often contradict their position by the causes they hold most dear. If social influence is not an extremely important factor in human behavior, then why spend so much time and effort in supporting Christian day schools, Christian colleges, missionary endeavors, or even the activities of the church?

There is still another dimension to the matter of the importance of the social factor in human behavior. The error of an "extreme behavioralism" that sees the individual only as a socially conditioned creature is that it misses half the story. Most sociological theory emphasizes not "social conditioning" but rather "social interaction." This means that the individual is viewed not only as socially influenced but also as socially influencing. The individual is not presented simply as a passive product of culture and social experience; he is presented also as a creature who has the potential to reflect on and evaluate culture and social experience. For sociology not to contain this emphasis would be naïve. If the human being is not capable of independent, critical thought, what is the source of new ideas? What is the source of social change? As the sociologist Peter Berger points out, persons who totally rationalize their behavior on the basis of social conditioning are acting in "bad faith."[25] They are denying their potential as thinking, responsible human beings.

Up to this point, our discussion has focused on how the scriptural message about the nature of human beings relates to the assumptions of the social sciences. In a sense, studying this relationship demands that Christian scholars, armed with scriptural principles, inform social-scientific theory. But I would like to turn the tables now and suggest that disciplines like sociology can also inform the Christian community. Sociology is concerned with the scientific study of how "human social behavior is organized and how this organization changes over time."[26] As a science, sociology attempts to understand the social world through the use of the human senses. The resulting observations serve as the basis for testing out general sociological explanations of the social world. The main difference between the scientific method of achieving knowledge and everyday common-sense approaches is that the former is more systematic, carried out according to specific rules and procedures that minimize error.

The focus of sociological interest is how social behavior is organized in human society. Human beings make an organized effort to achieve such tasks as producing and distributing economic goods, educating people for jobs, and controlling peoples' destructive behavior. These organized patterns of social behavior are varyingly referred to as a "social organization," a "social structure," or the "social order." For example, capitalism is the social structure according to which Americans have chosen to organize most of their economic activities. Moreover, the sociological interest is a dynamic one: sociologists are concerned with how social organization changes over time and what factors produce those changes.

Christians maintain that discipleship involves critical evaluation and often alteration of personal behavior according to biblical principles. They must hold the same attitude toward society's structures. Full discipleship demands that the Christian evangelical community consider the social structures of American society against the backdrop of Christian norms like justice, stewardship, and charity.[27]

Here sociology and the other social sciences are of value to Christians. They offer a systematic body of information about the character of society. With this, Christians can evaluate societal structures on a firmer basis than merely impressionistic evidence, common sense, or traditional cultural beliefs. In this book we will attempt to make a well-informed evaluation of the traditional sex-role structure of American society by bringing together biological, sociological, anthropological, and biblical evidence.

Discussion Questions

1/ In this chapter it has been argued that technological changes are blurring traditional female and male roles. Do you agree? Why or why not? Are other factors contributing to the blurring of these roles?

2/ Reflect on the social activities of the adult women and men you know well. Do their activities deviate from traditional male and female roles? If so, has this created problems for them?

3/ Do you think the tremendous increase in married women's participation in the labor force is a healthful or unhealthful development? Why?

4/ Employed wives tend to have more influence in family decision-making than nonemployed wives. Why do you think this is so?

5/ To what extent can Christians be comfortable with the goals and activities of the National Organization for Women as outlined in this chapter?

6/ Do you believe that the perspectives and data of the social sciences can be of value to Christians as they attempt to unravel the issues bearing on contemporary sex roles? Why or why not?

Suggested Readings

Berger, Peter L. Invitation to Sociology: A Humanistic Perspective. New York: Doubleday & Co., 1963.

A highly readable introduction to the major components of the sociological orientation. Although not written from a distinctively Christian perspective, it isolates the implications of the sociological enterprise in such a way that Christians can readily begin to determine how their faith relates to sociology.

Cavan, Ruth Shonle. **The American Family** New York: Thomas Y. Crowell Co., 1969.

Treats marriage and the family in American society from a sociological perspective. The first three chapters trace the historical trends that have given us the contemporary American family. Throughout these chapters Cavan pays careful attention to the major issues regarding husband-and-wife roles today.

Freeman, Jo, ed. **Women: A Feminist Perspective.** Palo Alto, California: Mayfield Publishing Co., 1975.

The title is somewhat misleading because it suggests a purely political statement. Although the conclusions of Freeman and her co-writers are consistent with a moderate feminist analysis of society, this anthology is largely a scholarly introductory treatment of the social-scientific data that bear on the status of women and men in society. It contains also some informative articles on the goals and accomplishments of the current feminist movement.

/2/

BIOLOGICAL DIFFER-
ENCES BETWEEN
THE SEXES

Women and men are two biologically separable sets of
human beings. The two sexes have biological heritages
that set the outside boundaries for their behavior. Anyone
who wishes to scrutinize traditional sex roles and suggest
possible changes must keep these biological differences
in mind. It is futile to require of either women or men
behavior that lies outside their biological potential.

Popular belief tells us that males, by virtue of their
biological heritage, are more "aggressive" and "stronger"
than females. This gives them an edge over females in
playing the provider role in a competitive job market and
better fits them for those roles requiring physical
strength. Women, on the other hand, are thought to be
biologically destined to be more "emotional" and "nurturant" than men. Therefore, the argument goes, they are
less equipped to handle the stress of competition in the

workaday world and better endowed to rear children. Many Americans, then, think the traditional division of labor between the sexes is realistic because it reflects what they believe are the biological natures of women and men.

Perhaps these prevailing cultural beliefs do not accurately reflect actual biological differences however. Perhaps they are partially unfounded stereotypes that have arisen to support traditional social practices. In this chapter we will review the evidence about biological differences between men and women.

Human Sexual Differentiation

How the human embryo develops into either a male or a female has long occupied the attention of researchers. A major figure among these researchers is Dr. John Money, a medical psychologist from the Johns Hopkins University. Dr. Money has spent more than twenty-five years investigating sexual differentiation and has reported his findings in books entitled *Man and Woman, Boy and Girl,* and *Sexual Signatures.*[1] Much of the following explanation of embryonic development is based on these books.

As soon as a child is born, it is identified as a girl or a boy on the basis of its external genital organs. However, the development of these organs was only one of what Money calls the "four major sex differentiation forks" that determined the gender of the fetus.[2]

The first fork in human sexual differentiation occurs at conception. An ovum (egg) produced by one of the mother's ovaries unites with one of the millions of sperm cells produced by the father's testes. The ovum and the sperm carry twenty-three chromosomes each, and each chromosome carries hundreds of genes that will govern various aspects of the child's development. At conception the ovum's chromosomes join up with the sperm's chromosomes to give the new cell twenty-three pairs. One of the twenty-three pairs determines the genetic sex. If both the mother and the father contributed an X chromosome to the sex-determining pair in the new cell, the child will be a chromosomal female (XX). On the other hand, if the mother's X-carrying ovum was fertilized by a sperm cell carrying a Y chromosome, the child will be a chromosomal male (XY). Since all ova have X chromosomes while sperm cells may carry either an X or a Y, chromosomal sex is determined by the sperm.

The timing must be right for conception to occur. The mother produces an ovum once a month. After its release from the ovary, an ovum lives only one day. A sperm cell survives only two days once it is in the mother's vagina, and then only if the chemical balance of the mother is right for it. The result is that only one out of every one hundred acts of sexual intercourse without contraception results in the fertilization of an egg.[3]

During the first month and a half after conception, XX and XY embryos develop in the same way. The embryo develops two gonads, which later will become either ovaries or testicles. Two sets of internal ducts appear also. One of these, called the mullerian structure, may eventually develop into the uterus, fallopian tubes, and upper vagina of a female. The other, called the wolffian structure, may later become the seminal vesicles, prostate gland, and vasa deferentia of a male. Externally, the embryo comes to look like a female. There is an opening surrounded by lip-like swellings; a protuberance of tissue at the head of the opening is known as a genital tubercle.[4]

At the end of the sixth week, the second fork in sexual differentiation is reached. If the embryo is a chromosomal male (XY), the Y chromosome sends a message to the two gonads instructing them to develop tubular structures and become testicles. But if the embryo is a chromosomal female (XX), no such instruction takes place, and the embryo's gonads remain in the same undeveloped state for another six weeks. At that point they begin to develop into ovaries, complete with egg cells; and this completes the second step in differentiation.

The sex chromosomes, then, play a significant role in early embryonic development by sending or not sending a message to the undifferentiated gonads. According to Money, once this is accomplished the sex chromosomes no longer play a direct part in human sexual differentiation.

Once the testicles are developed, they start to produce sex hormones. Three types of hormones are produced. The first is progesterone, commonly referred to as the "pregnancy hormone" because its level rises in a woman when she is pregnant. The second is androgen, often called the "male hormone" because its level is generally higher in men than in women. The third type of hormone is estrogen, the "female hormone," whose level is usually higher in women than men. Both women and men possess all three of these hormones. The difference is in proportions. In men, the testicles release sufficient androgen to dominate the estrogen produced, while in women the estrogen dominates the androgen.

At the third fork of human sexual differentiation, either the wolffian or the mullerian structure begins to develop further while the other one begins to atrophy. Prenatal hormone mix is the critical factor here. If the fetus has testicles and therefore is producing the male hormone mix, the wolffian structure is stimulated by the mix to develop into the seminal vesicles, prostate gland, and vasa deferentia of a male. Also, the male hormone mix at this point includes an additional hormonal substance that stops the mullerian structure from developing. If the fetus does not have the male hormone mix, the mullerian structure develops into a uterus, fallopian tubes, and upper vagina. At the same time the wolffian structure begins to wither away. Dr. Money points out that a female hormone mix is not necessary for the mullerian structure to develop and the wolffian structure to shrivel. Hormone production by the ovaries seems to be irrelevant for pre-natal differentiation along the female route; only the ab-sence of a male hormone mix is required.

The last fork in prenatal sexual differentiation among human beings comes after the chromosomal sex, gonadal sex (ovaries or testicles), and hormone mix have been determined. This last fork involves the development of the external genitals. Until then, both chromosomal male and chromosomal female embryos have the external geni-tals described earlier—an opening surrounded by lip-like swellings, with a protuberance of tissue (the genital tubercle) at the mouth of the opening. Thereafter, de-pending again on the hormone mix, the fetus develops along the female or male route.

As with female development of the mullerian structure and withering of the wolffian structure, female molding of the external genitals needs no hormone stimulus. In the absence of a male hormone mix, the embryo's open-ing differentiates into two, the vaginal opening and the urethral opening. The genital tubercle remains small to become a clitoris, and the lip-like swellings differentiate into labia majora.

If the embryo has the male hormone mix, the genital tubercle grows into a penis. The lip-like swellings join together to form the scrotum, into which the testicles later descend. The seam along the back of the developed male's scrotum is evidence of this prenatal male genital molding.

Reflection on the four major forks in human prenatal sexual differentiation reveals some interesting points. First, once the chromosomal sex of the embryo has been established as XX or XY at conception, the embryo devel-ops along the female route unless it is stimulated otherwise. The Y chromosome must send a specific message to the gonads to differentiate as testicles; otherwise they will develop as ovaries. No message is needed from an X chromosome for the gonads to differentiate into ovaries. Similarly, the male hormone mix along with a special mullerian-inhibiting substance must be present in order for the wolffian structure to realize its potential as internal male genitals. No special hormone mix is needed for the mullerian structure to develop into female genitals; all that is required is the absence of the male hormone mix. Finally, the external genitals are molded as female or male simply on the basis of the absence or the presence of the male hormone mix; the female hormone mix does not have a direct effect on this molding. Money summarizes the principle in this way: "Unless there is a sufficient push in the male direction, the fetus will take the female turn at any subsequent fork, whether there is a female push or not."[5]

Reflection on prenatal sexual differentiation yields a second important point. Although a newborn's sex is generally ascertained at birth by the appearance of the external genitals, this is only one of the four bases for determining sex. The other three are the newborn's chromosomal sex (XX or XY), gonadal sex (ovaries or testicles), and hormone mix (estrogen-dominated or androgen-dominated). Once in a while these various bases for a person's sex may be at odds with one another. For example, a chromosomal and gonadal male whose testicles produce sufficient androgen for male fetal development may be incapable of using that androgen; being insensitive to androgen, the wolffian structure and external genitals of the fetus do not develop along the male route. Yet the mullerian-inhibiting substance does operate. As a result, the person is born with the chromosomes and gonads of a male, the developed internal genitals of neither sex, and the external genitals of a female, which will probably lead to an F on the birth certificate and the social training normally given a girl. Individuals having this and other sexually ambiguous biological makeups are called hermaphrodites.[6]

After birth there are two significant alterations in the biological functioning of both sexes, one at puberty and the other much later in life. The biological functions that are started with the first alteration (at puberty) are slowed down or stopped at the second.

Puberty is not a single event but rather a process that occurs over a period of years. At about the age of nine or ten, the pituitary gland, which is located in the brain, begins to secrete certain hormones that in turn stimulate the gonads to increase their hormone production. Androgen levels go up in both sexes, but far more in boys. Estrogen production increases considerably in girls. The increased level of sex hormones initiates a growth surge and the development of secondary sex characteristics. In girls, the breasts develop, pubic hair appears, the hip bones spread, and the subcutaneous layer of fat thickens in a pattern that rounds out the body. In boys, facial hair and pubic hair appear, muscle and bone mass noticeably increase, and the larynx enlarges, which deepens the voice. The sex organs start growing in both sexes. Later on, girls begin to ovulate and menstruate, while the prostate gland of boys develops fluid and the testicles begin to produce mature sperm.

This biological functioning that is necessary for human reproduction continues well into adulthood. After a number of decades, however, further change takes place. By late middle age, women enter the period called menopause, when they experience a sudden decline in the functioning of the ovaries. Ovulation ceases, and the ovaries' production of both estrogen and androgen falls off sharply. Because estrogen levels are now lower and because the adrenal gland, another source of androgen, continues to produce this male hormone, menopause brings about a certain masculinization in women. There is an increase in the growth of facial hair, the body shape becomes less round, the breasts lose their fullness, and a tendency toward baldness sets in.[7] No such dramatic change in biological functioning occurs in men. Rather, their androgen level decreases only slowly with the aging process, and their testicles may continue to produce healthy sperm for the rest of their lives. Because estrogen levels in adult men generally do not change while androgen levels decrease with age, some feminization of the body may occur in old men.[8]

This information about prenatal human sexual differentiation and the significant alterations in biological functioning after birth serves as a basis from which to examine common cultural beliefs about the biological differences between women and men.

On "Strength" and the Sexes

A prevalent cultural belief in America is that men are "the stronger sex." Male athletes run and swim faster than women. They high-jump higher and broad-jump farther. And if the implements are of similar weight, men toss the shot put, discus, and javelin farther than women. Thus, it is argued, in sports where muscular strength is important, men clearly show that they are the stronger sex.

Some people have argued that the difference in physical strength between women and men is due more to cultural than to biological factors. Ann Crittenden Scott, for instance, points out that American culture contains certain beliefs about women and strenuous physical activity: "athletics will masculinize a woman's appearance," "sports are aggressive and therefore 'unfeminine,'" "women are more easily injured than men," and women should not engage in strenuous physical activity while menstruating or pregnant because physical problems might result.[9] These beliefs, Scott argues, have served to keep girls and women off the playing field and away from other forms of strenuous physical activity. The result is a much wider gap between the peak physical performances of women and men than their biological potential seems to necessitate. As evidence for this, Scott points to the faster rate of improvement in the Olympic performances of women than men in this century, the data showing that the gap in strength between physically conditioned male and female athletes is considerably less than the gap in strength between average men and women, and the fact that "the differences of strength within either sex are far greater than the differences between them."[10]

While Scott's basic argument has considerable merit, it is highly unlikely that similar physical-training programs from birth on could ever result in the same average levels of physical strength for the two sexes. There appear to be obvious biological reasons why men have greater physical strength than women. Men have more bone mass, more muscle, and less fat. Fifty-two percent of the average man's body weight is muscle, or lean body mass, while only 40 percent of the average woman's body weight is lean body mass.[11] Although some of this difference in lean body mass is due to different levels of physical activity, the difference can hardly be attributed wholly to this source. Prior to puberty there is not a great difference in size and strength between girls and boys. At puberty, however, boys experience a much greater increase in the production of androgen than girls, and this influences the development of muscle tissue and bone mass. Girls, on the other hand, develop an estrogen-dominated hormone mix that brings about the thickening of the subcutaneous layer of fat. In addition, some of the difference is due simply to the larger size of men.[12]

The difference in strength between men and women can be traced not only to differences in physique but also to differences in physiological support systems. Men have larger hearts, greater lung capacity, a higher percentage of red blood cells (which carry oxygen), and a higher hemoglobin content in those cells (hemoglobin carries oxygen from the lungs to the tissues, and carbon dioxide from the tissues to the lungs). These differences combine to give men a greater potential for energy output. That is, for a given amount of physical work, women have to operate closer to their maximum than men. Moreover, the heat tolerance of men is greater than that of women. Because women have proportionately fewer sweat glands and their subcutaneous layer of fat acts as an insulator, keeping body heat in, women sweat less readily than men. The evaporation of sweat is the mechanism by which the body is cooled, and so women have a lower heat tolerance.[13]

But there is another way in which to approach the question of which sex is stronger. "Strength" may be defined not only in terms of lean muscle mass and power output but also in terms of survival potential. Here the focus is on the traits that enhance a person's chances for living a long life. In this regard women appear to be more richly endowed biologically and hence the "stronger" sex.

At every stage of life, males die off at a higher rate than females. Although fathers produce as many X sperm as Y sperm, estimates of miscarriage indicate that there are perhaps as many as 140 conceptions of males for every 100 conceptions of females.[14] By birth, the ratio has fallen to 106 males for every 100 females, and at the end of the first year of life, the ratio has dropped further to 105 males to 100 females. The same trend continues throughout childhood, so that by puberty there are 102 males to

100 females. During early adulthood the sex ratio equalizes, and later females pull ahead. By the early seventies there are 106 females to 100 males, and at age ninety there are 150 females to 100 males. These data are often cited as an indication that females are constitutionally stronger than males.

Other observers disagree. They point out that American society both directly and indirectly encourages boys to be more aggressive, to play in rougher, more dangerous ways than girls. (It is true that during childhood and adolescence, the accident rate is higher for males than for females, just as it is during later stages of life.) In adulthood men take on combat duty in wars. They are expected to make their way in a highly competitive job market. They are constantly subjected to the stress associated with providing for the economic security of their families. And society burdens men rather than women with the more hazardous, life-shortening occupations. No wonder, the argument goes, more males than females die off at every stage of life.

Some of the points of this argument are certainly open to question. But even if this were not so, the argument still would not adequately account for the sex-ratio data. The argument ignores the fact that the 40 percent advantage of males at conception drops to only a 6 percent advantage at birth. It would hardly seem possible that social or cultural factors could account for why more male fetuses die in the prenatal environment. Pregnant women are not more or less careful depending on whether they are carrying a culturally defined "weaker girl" or "stronger boy"; most of them have no idea of the sex of the fetus within them. Moreover, there is no apparent embryological reason why the prenatal environment should be more dangerous for males than females. At present, then, the evidence seems to indicate that males are constitutionally weaker than females.

There is additional evidence that fetal females are constitutionally stronger than fetal males. The sex-ratio data for conception and birth referred to earlier are for the United States. They are fairly consistent with data from other societies that have similar levels of nutrition and general health. However, data from societies that are poorer and have lower nutritional and health levels indicate that though the conception rates for females and males are probably the same as in the United States, the sex ratio at birth is even less in favor of males. For instance, in India 99 boys are born for every 100 girls, a 1 percent disadvantage for boys rather than the 6 percent advantage they have in the United States.[15] Similarly, the sex-ratio advantage of boys at birth in the United States is greater today than it was at the turn of the century, when nutritional and health standards were lower. In other words, the poorer the conditions, the higher the mortality rate of male fetuses relative to female fetuses. This again suggests that females are constitutionally stronger than males—that is, better equipped to survive under less than ideal health conditions.

The apparent greater constitutional strength of females is traceable in part to the chromosome difference between the sexes. The male has a Y chromosome; the female does not. The Y chromosome is much smaller than the X, and although the Y carries some valuable genetic information, it also transmits some that is undesirable.[16] Four diseases have been linked to genes that are carried only by the Y chromosome and hence can be transmitted only from father to son. These are ichthyosis hystrix gravior (barklike skin), hypertrichosis (a dense, hairy growth on the ears), keratom dissipatum (hard lesions of the hands and feet), and a webbing of the second and third toes.

Yet the biological disadvantages attached to having a Y chromosome and hence to being a male result not so much from the genes that the Y chromosome carries as from what it does not carry. Hemophilia, often called bleeder's disease, illustrates this point well. The cause of this genetically transmitted disorder is a single sex-linked recessive gene. The hemophilia gene is linked to the X chromosome and, being recessive, will not express itself if there is an opposite X chromosome with a normal gene. Therefore, when an X chromosome carrying the hemophilia gene is genetically passed on to a female, it is very unlikely that she will get hemophilia because the chances are slim that her other X chromosome will be carrying this recessive gene also. But a male's Y chromosome cannot suppress the effects of the recessive hemophilia gene. If a male receives an X chromosome bearing the hemophilia gene, he will get the disease. As a result, by far the majority of hemophiliacs are males who received the hemophilia gene from their mothers.

In addition to hemophilia, more than sixty other disorders that occur primarily in males are known to be linked to genes carried by the X chromosome. Among them are albinism of the eyes, total congenital cataract, color blindness of the red-green type, congenital deafness, epidermal cysts, certain forms of mental deficiency, myopia, and Parkinsonism.[17] For a male to get them, only the mother has to be a carrier; for a female to get them, both parents must be carriers.

Data on illnesses that are not known to be sex-linked suggest that women have a greater ability to fight disease and hence are constitutionally stronger. Even though after puberty women have a higher illness rate than men, women recover from diseases much more frequently than men. Death from practically all forms of disease at all ages is more common for men than women. The only illnesses from which women die more frequently than men are those directly related to their reproductive systems, and a few others such as chorea and whooping cough.[18]

The precise influence of various social and biological factors on sex differences in disease and mortality rates is not known. The only way to determine this would be to select matched groups of healthy females and males at birth, subject both groups to the same social pressures and task obligations, and measure their disease and mortality rates until all members of the groups had died. Aside from the cost, such research would certainly be unethical because of the extent to which the subjects' lives would have to be manipulated from birth until death.

There have been, however, some interesting research findings about this question of the influence of social and biological factors on the mortality rates of men and women. Francis Madigan, attempting to find matched groups of males and females, obtained mortality rates from nearly ten thousand Catholic brothers and more than thirty thousand Catholic sisters engaged in educational work from 1900 to the mid-fifties.[19] By focusing on these religious workers, Madigan says, he removed five very significant sources of differential stress that have been cited as causes of the higher mortality rates of men: (1) male service in the armed forces, (2) greater male liberty to indulge in life-harming habits, (3) the different roles of husbands and wives, (4) the larger employment of males in dangerous and life-shortening occupations, and (5) the employment of women and men in different occupations. The same sort of difference in mortality rates was found: brothers died earlier than sisters. Madigan concluded that females have a greater life expectancy than males because of biological rather than social and cultural factors.

The matter of which is the stronger sex therefore depends upon how strength is defined. In terms of muscle and bone mass, males are stronger; in terms of the capacity to fight disease and death, females are stronger.

On "Aggression" and the
Sexes

Men are popularly believed to be more aggressive than women. This supposed inborn trait is often used to explain why men hold the major share of leadership positions in most known societies. Given the male's biological heritage, the rationale goes, he cannot help being dominant over the female.[20] Similarly, when it comes to playing the provider role in a modern society with its highly competitive economic system, men are thought to have a decided edge over women in handling the obligations and stresses of this role.

The term "aggression" is difficult to define because it is used to refer to many different kinds of behavior. Behaviors as different as murder, a junior executive's working his way to the top, and a student's attempting to outargue a knowledgeable professor may be labeled aggressive. It is no surprise, then, that social scientists have not been fully consistent in how they define this concept. Still, there is one main idea running through most of the definitions: aggressive behavior is intended to harm another person in some way.[21]

Given this stipulation, the evidence from behavioral studies indicates that males are the more aggressive sex.[22] This general finding holds from preschool years on into adulthood. Observational and experimental studies of preschoolers reveal that boys hit, aggressively wrestle, "mock fight" (play rough), and verbally insult their peers more than girls do. Boys are also more likely than girls to fight back if they have been either verbally or physically attacked. Limited cross-cultural research shows that the same patterns hold for young children in different types of societies.[23]

The major share of psychological research on aggression from early childhood into adulthood involves placing subjects in a contrived situation in which there is an opportunity to behave aggressively. In many of these studies, subjects first observe others behaving both aggressively and nonaggressively, and then the subject's own behavior is observed for signs of aggression. In others, subjects are told that they are helping the experimenter teach someone else a particular task by administering electric shocks to that person when he makes mistakes. (The person being "taught" is not actually shocked, but the subjects learn this only after the experiment.) Results of the majority of these studies consistently show that males are more likely than females to behave aggressively after observing aggressive behavior and that, for the most part, they administer higher levels of shock as well as shocks of longer duration.

It might be argued that the sexes are equally prone toward aggressive behavior and that the reason for a difference between the sexes in the research evidence is that males have been encouraged to display such behavior whereas females have been taught it is inappropriate for them. There is also the possibility that the sexes have been taught to express their aggressive impulses in different ways. Perhaps females have to show their aggressive hostility in more subtle ("catty") ways. Having summarized the large body of social scientific and biological data on this matter, Eleanor Maccoby and Carol Jacklin conclude that although the social environment most certainly influences the relative aggressiveness of women and men, the evidence still clearly suggests a biologically based difference between the sexes in threshold for aggression.[24] That is, given the same stimulation toward aggressive behavior, males are more biologically predisposed to respond aggressively than females.

What is the biological basis for this difference between men and women? The evidence on this point—most of which is from experiments with animals—indicates that aggression is related to hormone mix.[25] To date, research has linked hormones to aggression in three ways.

The first link between hormones and aggression is at the prenatal stage of development. Earlier in this chapter it was pointed out that androgen functions prenatally to masculinize the growing fetus. Experiments with monkeys have shown that if testosterone (the most active type of androgen) is administered to pregnant monkeys, the female offspring not only have masculinized genitals but also are more likely than nonandrogenized females to engage in rough-and-tumble play and other forms of physical aggression. For obvious reasons, similar experiments cannot be carried out on human beings, but there are a few parallel cases among human beings where chromosomal females received excessive amounts of androgen prenatally because of abnormal functioning of the fetus's adrenal glands or because of injections containing male hormones that were given to the pregnant mother. These fetally androgenized girls engaged in somewhat more aggressive fighting behavior than a matched group of fetally nonandrogenized girls, but not so much as normal boys. Apparently, then, prenatal androgenization is related to lowering the threshold for aggressive behavior in females, but it certainly is not sufficient to bring the threshold down to the level of males.

Postnatal hormone mix is also tied to the threshold for aggressive behavior. Experiments with animals ranging from chickens to monkeys indicate that testosterone administered to females after birth increases their fighting behavior. Some female monkeys who had been physically dominated by males physically subdued the males after they were injected with testosterone. It is still an open question whether an increase in testosterone level in human females will increase their threshold for physical aggression.

A third way in which researchers have attempted to

link hormones and aggression is by examining whether the level of testosterone in the male bloodstream is directly related to the degree of aggression. Research on monkey troupes has shown that the males with the highest testosterone levels dominated the troupes through physical fighting. Limited research with men in prison revealed that a high testosterone level was predictive of violent or aggressive crimes but was not related to verbal aggression or fighting behavior while in prison. These findings, however, must be interpreted with care. Testosterone level fluctuates with experience. If, for instance, an animal wins a fight, his testosterone level is high. If he is defeated, his testosterone level decreases. At the present stage of research, it appears that a high concentration of testosterone can be both a cause and an effect of aggressive behavior.

Although the evidence is not definitive, it certainly suggests a biological basis for the greater aggressiveness of men. Yet one must be extremely careful in drawing inferences from this conclusion. First, most of the evidence comes from animal studies, and there are obvious hazards in extending these findings to human beings. (What little evidence there is about human beings, however, is consistent with the animal studies.) Second, to acknowledge men as the more aggressive sex does not mean that women are not aggressive. Women, like men, have the potential to inflict all sorts of harm on others. Third, there is not a one-to-one relation between a male hormone mix and a high level of aggression.

All studies measuring aggression and sex find that there are always a considerable number of women who are more aggressive than a considerable number of men. What the evidence does indicate, then, is that those with male hormone mix generally require slightly less of a stimulus to engage in aggressive behavior. Once over the threshold, aggression is mediated by other factors such as age, health, strength, cultural values, and social experience.

The research findings on aggression are perhaps even more significantly qualified if they are considered in the light of data on psychological characteristics commonly associated with aggression. When men are tagged the more aggressive sex, this means to many that men are also more competitive and more dominant. By implication, women are thought to be more timid and compliant. Examining the research evidence on each of these psychological attributes, Maccoby and Jacklin found that sex differences on each are still an open question. The research findings are contradictory or indicate basically no difference between the sexes in regard to these attributes. Seemingly, the biological foundation for the sex difference in thresholds for physical and verbal aggression does not similarly affect thresholds for competition, timidity, or compliance.

Overall, then, the argument that men are better fitted for the provider role in a competitive economy because they are more aggressive seems to be blown out of proportion. There is a biologically based difference between the sexes in aggression only if aggression is defined as physical or verbal action intended to threaten or harm another. While this type of behavior is important for achieving dominance in troupes of monkeys or even young children, it is hardly a culturally approved mode of behavior among adults. Perhaps this in part accounts for why aggression so defined declines with age in both sexes. At any rate, advancement in the occupational world rarely depends on physical aggression. Success and leadership are more likely to be based on intelligence, hard work, persuasion, cooperation, bargaining, and at times the more unsavory nonaggressive techniques of flattery, bribery, and deception.

On "Emotionality," "Nur-
turance," and the Sexes

Women have been thought to be less suited for the provider role not only because they are believed to be less aggressive than men but also because they are considered more "emotional." Supposedly being subject to more emotional ups and downs, they are less able to handle the stress associated with providing economic support for the family. This belief, coupled with the notion that women are more biologically prone toward nurturant behavior, is often used as the basis for arguing that women should stay out of the labor force and remain at home, caring for the needs of their children.

It is true that many women have predictable changes in their emotional states resulting from a biological phenomenon that men do not have, the menstrual cycle. During the female cycle there are shifts in hormone levels.[26]. Estrogen is at a low level at the beginning of the cycle. It rises until it reaches a high point at ovulation or midcycle, dips, rises again, and finally falls sharply just before the onset of menstruation.

Researchers have linked these hormonal shifts in women to predictable changes in emotional states.[27] During the few days before menstruation when estrogen and progesterone levels have dropped, from 24 to 100 percent of women (the proportion varies considerably depending on the sensitivity of the measuring instrument) experience "premenstrual tension," that is, a rise in feelings of irritability, hostility, depression, and anxiety. In one of the more careful studies of premenstrual tension, researchers Bardwick and Ivery asked normal women at different points in their menstrual cycles to describe their recent experiences. Using a psychological scoring device, the researchers found that the accounts given by the subjects at the time of premenstruation often referred to death, separation, and anxiety. Accounts given at the time of ovulation showed considerably more self-satisfaction. Bardwick and Ivery concluded that "general psychological mood-states correlated with menstrual cycle phases."[28]

As further evidence for premenstrual tension, Katherina Dalton collected data showing that certain behaviors occur at a higher rate during the four premenstrual days and the four menstrual days.[29] Her research showed that among women, 46 percent of admissions to mental hospitals, 53 percent of attempted suicides, 45 percent of sick leaves by industrial employees, 52 percent of emergency admissions to hospitals because of accidents, and 49 percent of crimes committed by prisoners occurred during the premenstrual and menstrual days. On the basis of chance, these figures should be around 25 percent.

The physiological changes accompanying menopause have also been cited as a part of the biological basis for women's greater emotionality. Along with the decline in the functioning of the ovaries and the resulting lower level of estrogen production come a number of both psychological and psychosomatic symptoms.[30] Many women are irritable, unable to concentrate, confused, anxious, and depressed; psychosomatically, the symptoms of headaches, dizzy spells, and heart pounding are common. It is estimated that from 50 to 85 percent of women experience these symptoms at menopause, though the severity varies considerably.

Since the male does not experience anything similar to the female's menstrual cycle, he is commonly thought to be more emotionally stable. This conclusion is simplistic. The fact that many women are more irritable, anxious, and depressed at certain times than at others does not necessarily mean they are more emotional than men. In fact, in reviewing the research on various measures of emotionality, Maccoby and Jacklin do not find consistent sex differences.[31] And though it is true that female rates of suicide, admission to mental hospitals, accidents, and crime are disproportionately high during the four premenstrual and four menstrual days, still, in each category, male rates far exceed female rates. Finally, those fluctuations in mood that are due to the menstrual cycle and menopause can be largely controlled through estrogen therapy. When women are taking birth-control pills containing estrogen, their hormone levels remain relatively constant throughout the menstrual cycle, and so do their levels of anxiety and hostility. Estrogen is also frequently prescribed for women who are experiencing the symptoms accompanying menopause.[32]

Not only are women commonly believed to be more emotional than men, but they are also thought to be more prone toward nurturant behavior and thus better fitted to care for children. Nurturance, like aggression, is a slippery term, but a common element runs through most definitions of it. Nurturant behavior is the giving of aid or comfort to someone who is younger, weaker, or for some other reason in a dependent position relative to the nurturant person.[33]

Whether or not there is a biological basis for women's being the more nurturant sex is not yet fully clear. Anthropologist Lionel Tiger maintains that mothers are more predisposed toward the nurturing of children because of the long and intimate physiological relationship a pregnant woman has with her gestating child.[34] However, Tiger admits he has little empirical support for this position. A few animal studies suggest that the hormones associated with pregnancy predispose the female toward taking care of her young. For instance, when blood plasma is taken from female rats who have recently given birth and is given to virgin female rats, the latter, when given pups, will show maternal behavior such as retrieving pups, building a nest, and licking pups more quickly than untreated virgin females.[35] No comparable experimental evidence about human beings or even monkeys is available. What data there are on the maternal behavior of monkeys indicate that a prenatal male hormone mix can raise the threshold for the later release of nurturant behavior toward the young.[36] Prenatally androgenized (masculinized) female monkeys need more stimulation to care for baby monkeys than do normal female monkeys. The few human genetic females who were prenatally androgenized show a similar pattern. Money and Ehrhardt found that girls who had been fetally androgenized were less interested in playing with dolls and less interested in caring for younger children than a control group made up of their own normal sisters.[37]

Certainly the research bearing on the belief that women are the more nurturant sex is less than impressive. There has not been the controlled experimentation that would justify such a belief. Yet even if future research bears out the fragmentary evidence we now have, we need to remember that only a very minor difference between the sexes will have been shown. Money and Tucker have pointed out that a difference in prenatal hormone mix means only "a slight difference" in the threshold for the release of nurturant behavior. The evidence in no way suggests a qualitative difference between the sexes in the type of nurturant behavior they exhibit. In other words, once the threshold for nurturant behavior has been crossed, both sexes appear to be equally proficient at the behavior. Male rats are as proficient at licking and retrieving rat pups as female rats who have just given birth; it just takes the males somewhat longer to get started doing it. The same holds true for male and female rhesus monkeys,[38] as well as for fetally androgenized human females and normal ones.

On "Human Sexuality"
and the Sexes

For the greater share of the twentieth century, a typically Freudian perspective has served as the basis for much of the popular thinking about human sexuality.[39] According to this, sex, in its most fundamental terms, is an instinctive biological drive, the aim of which is to release tension and thereby bring pleasure or satisfaction. This innate biological drive is generally thought to be stronger in men than in women. Hence, in this as well as in other areas of life, men are considered more aggressive—that is, more active in seeking out or initiating a sexual relationship—while women are believed to be more passive and dependent.

Although definitive data on the biological basis for the sex drive are lacking, what clinical and presumptive evidence there is suggests that sex hormones again may play a role.[40] Men who are given estrogen (the "female hormone") sometimes seem to have their sexual desire reduced.[41] In fact, estrogen has sometimes been used in an attempt to suppress the sex drive of habitual sex offenders.[42] On the other hand, androgen (the "male hormone") seems to increase sexual desire in some women. Also, depriving men of androgen by removing the testicles eventually results in, among other things, a decrease in sexual desire. If male castrates are given androgen therapy, their sexual desire tends to return.[43] These findings are usually taken as evidence that androgen is the libido hormone in both sexes, and that, since men have a larger amount of androgen in circulation, men are destined to be more sexually aggressive.

Yet the relation of sex hormones to libido drive is not a simple one. Many men do not experience a reduction in sex drive when given estrogen, nor do all women experience an increase in sex drive when given androgen. Moreover, the amount of time elapsing between castration and the loss of sex drive varies greatly in men—from weeks to years.[44] Nor does a cross-cultural perspective on the sex drive reveal that men are inevitably the sexual aggressors. In some societies, women are more aggressive in initiating sexual relationships, and in others, no distinction is made between the sexes in this matter.[45]

Because hormone mix does not adequately account for how strong the sexual drive is or which sex initiates the sexual relationship, recent analysts have begun to emphasize the importance of social learning in human sexuality. For example, after completing an extensive cross-cultural study of patterns of human sexual behavior, researchers Ford and Beach concluded that the kinds of stimulation that can produce sexual excitement are largely learned, and that the behavior through which this excitement is expressed depends largely upon the individual's past experiences.[46]

Do men, then, by virtue of their biology, have a stronger sex drive than women, and are they innately more sexually aggressive than women? This question cannot be accurately answered yet; the evidence is too scanty. However, we do know that the Freudian view of human sexuality as being purely instinctive is too simplistic. Most aspects of human sexuality, sex drive and sexual aggression included, are governed by social learning as well as by biology.

Conclusion

In this chapter we have reviewed a considerable body of biological evidence about the differences between women and men. Although the research is not as definitive as we would like, the overall impression that emerges is that the popular beliefs about the biological differences greatly exaggerate them. Men generally are physically stronger than women, but they also are constitutionally weaker. Men appear to have a lower threshold for aggressive behavior than women, but only when aggression is defined as physical or verbal behavior intended to harm another, a type of behavior generally not socially valued in adults. The female monthly cycle can be linked to changes in psychological moods in many women, but on culturally accepted measures of emotional weakness (mental-illness rates and suicide rates) men rank higher than women. There is only slight suggestive evidence that women's threshold for nurturant behavior is a bit lower than men's. Finally, though this has not been fully researched, it is possible that sex drive is somewhat stronger in men than in women. However, that drive is also influenced by social learning.

One would be hard put to argue on the basis of this evidence that men are biologically destined to be providers while women are biologically programmed to care for children and the household. Admittedly, the biological research is not definitive; perhaps other biological differences between the sexes are yet to be discovered. However, the research that has been done has failed to find clear biological differences that would better fit the sexes for certain tasks or roles in society rather than others.

Perhaps it is time to rephrase the question with which we approach the literature on biological differences. Instead of asking, "Is there any evidence that men are biologically more suited to be providers while women are biologically better fitted to care for a home and children?," we should ask: "What is the potential of women and of men for accomplishing the various tasks in society?" Asking the first question often leads to an overemphasis—even to the point of distortion—on the minor differences discussed in this chapter. The second question would probably result in a more balanced perspective on the biological heritages of men and women. It opens our eyes to the vast amount of potential that the sexes share as well as to the minor differences. Both sexes have the biological potential for a full range of human emotions and behavior—loving, hating, being rational, being irrational, being creative, being uncreative, being active, being dominant, being subordinate, being competitive, being noncompetitive, and so on. In the matter of potential for accomplishing various tasks in society, there are many more biological similarities than differences between women and men.

This is not to say that there are not major biological differences. There are obvious differences in reproductive roles: only women can menstruate, gestate, and lactate, and only men can impregnate.[47] No amount of social learning can transfer these functions from one sex to the other; they are biological imperatives. But beyond these, scientific research has not uncovered anything in the biological heritages of men and women that would necessarily destine them for the tasks traditionally assigned to each in American society.

If the cultural beliefs about biological differences between women and men that have been used to justify traditional sex roles are largely unfounded, then how did a division of labor by sex arise in the first place? The next chapter deals with this question of the origin of sex roles.

Discussion Questions

1/ Does the greater constitutional strength of women better fit them for certain activities in society? If so, which ones? Has American society traditionally assigned these activities to women? Why or why not?

2/ In what kinds of occupations would the greater physical strength of men be an asset? Do these occupations make up a large proportion of the total number of occupations in American society? Are they prestigious or high-paying occupations?

3/ Has the information discussed in this chapter changed any of your views about the basic natures of women and men? If so, in what ways?

4/ Do people who believe there are major differences in the biological natures of men and women also tend to believe that women are inferior? If so, why?

5/ How well informed are most people about the actual biological differences between the sexes? Do you think that greater knowledge might cause the common conceptions of femininity and masculinity to change?

6/ Purely on the basis of the biological evidence, are there any social tasks that you would assign primarily to one sex or the other? If so, which ones and why?

7/ What implications does the biological evidence have for coed sports? Are there any athletic activities where it is feasible for men and women to participate on an equal basis on the same team?

Suggested Readings

Bardwick, Judith M. **Psychology of Women: A Study of Bio-Cultural Conflicts.** New York: Harper & Row, Publishers, 1971.

Written in part as a a response to prevalent Freudian notions about the nature of women. Bardwick focuses on the character of woman's reproductive system and its implications for her personality and social behavior.

Gerber, Ellen W., Jan Felshin, Pearl Berlin, and Waneen Wyrick. **The American Woman in Sport.** Reading, Massachusetts: Addison-Wesley Publishing Co., 1974.

An informative account of the various physiological systems operative in different forms of athletic activity. Throughout, attention is given to male-female differences. The reader gains a much better understanding of the biological differences between the sexes.

Maccoby, Eleanor Emmons, and Carol Nagy Jacklin. **The Psychology of Sex Differences.** Stanford: Stanford University Press, 1974.

An ambitious and well-executed compendium of research evidence bearing on the psychological differences between the sexes. The authors continually ponder the influence of biological and social factors on the psychological differences they discuss.

Money, John, and Patricia Tucker. **Sexual Signatures: On Being a Man or a Woman.** Boston: Little, Brown & Co., 1975.

A nontechnical adaptation of much of Dr. Money's research into the biological processes involved in sexual differentiation, both before and after birth. Money and Tucker have done an admirable job of sorting out the facts from the mass of cultural stereotypes regarding the biological natures of men and women. The book will almost certainly alter the reader's notions about the basis of feminine and masculine identities.

Montagu, Ashley. **The Natural Superiority of Women.** New York: Macmillan Publishing Co., 1974.

Contains a wealth of interesting and provocative data about the biological differences between men and women. However, the reader must take care with Montagu's interpretations of the evidence; he often goes well beyond what the data warrant.

/3/

THE ORIGIN OF TRAD-
ITIONAL SEX ROLES

The biological evidence discussed in the previous chapter raises the following questions: If the traditional roles of men and women are not firmly grounded in their God-created biological differences, then why is it that every known human society includes such sex roles as part of its social structure? Is there a biological basis for sex roles in some societies and not in others, or are sex roles inevitably a matter of social learning? In short, how did sex roles get started in the first place?

Scripture does not fully answer these questions, and again we must turn to the findings of social science to gain a more complete perspective. But first we need to look at some fundamental ideas about social organization and social roles.

Societal Organization
by Status and Role

The starting point for social organization may be found

in the fact that every society must accomplish certain tasks, such as rearing children, meeting the biological needs of its members, and maintaining order. Human societies never leave these tasks to the caprices of individual initiative. Rather, they divide up the tasks so that an orderly, collective effort is made to accomplish them.

To describe this phenomenon of social organization, sociologists have introduced the concepts of status and role.[1] Societies get tasks accomplished in an orderly way by assigning various categories of people to certain statuses—that is, certain positions in society—and attaching to these statuses various roles, or expectations for behavior. (In common usage, one's "status" is one's rank in society. Sociologists use the term more generally to refer to a person's various positions in society's structure; in addition to social-class status, one has age status, marital status, kinship status, and the like.)

For instance, American society accomplishes the general task of "higher education" of its youth by differentiating a number of status and role combinations that make up the social organization of the college or graduate school. Most colleges differentiate the statuses of members of the board of trustees, president of the college, deans, registrar, professors, students, secretaries, .and maintenance workers. Associated with each of these statuses is a role, a set of expectations for behavior. The role includes the more specific tasks that a person in that status is required to accomplish. The trustees are expected to make the major policy decisions affecting the college; the president is responsible for putting these decisions into effect and serves as chief liaison officer between the board of trustees and the college community; professors are expected to communicate the content of their areas of expertise in the classroom; and so on. By dividing up labor through the use of various status-role combinations, the college makes sure that an organized, collective effort is made to accomplish its primary task: higher education.

It is helpful to think of society as being organized in the same sense that a college is organized. However, the bases for assigning people to status-role combinations are far more extensive in society at large than in a college. People play different roles in the college on the basis of their formal education and their occupational skills. Society in general uses these two criteria for role assignment but many others as well. For instance, American society also uses age, race, religion, ethnic affiliation, and sex as bases for role assignment. The total pattern of status-role combinations in a given society constitutes the social organization of that society.

Interestingly, a cross-cultural analysis reveals that only two bases for role differentiation are used universally. These are age and sex. Every known society expects young and old people to play different roles and also assigns different roles to women and men. The probable reason is that though it is possible to conceive of a society that is homogeneous in race, religion, ethnic affiliation, or formal education, it is not possible to conceive of a society that is homogeneous in age or sex. Every society has always had people of different ages and different sexes, and every society has used these differences as bases on which to assign roles. For this reason, anthropologists cite age and sex as the most fundamental bases of social organization.

There is another facet to this process of role differentiation. The "expectations for behavior"—that is, the role—include more than just the tasks assigned to people holding that particular status. Once a society has determined which categories of people (judging by age, sex, race, and the like) ought to accomplish which tasks, it goes on to develop portraits of what these people are like. That is, society develops stereotyped conceptions of the attributes of people assigned different tasks in society. These role attributes are usually thought to be grounded in the biological heritage of the people concerned; hence they are used to explain why certain people should perform particular tasks in society.

A clear illustration of this can be found in the "black role" in American society. Historically, society has felt that blacks were best fitted for the more menial tasks such as cleaning buildings and for positions in the entertainment world and in professional sports. Society justified this task assignment by stereotyping blacks as innately less ambitious, less intelligent, more rhythmical, and more athletic than whites.

In summary, social roles are made up of two parts: a task component and an attribute component. By assigning different tasks to people occupying different statuses, society ensures that there will be an organized attempt to reach its main goals. In this sense, roles are the building blocks of a society's social order. In addition, by stereotyping the attributes of people working at various tasks, society provides itself with a ready-made rationale for its division of labor whenever that division is challenged.

Sex-Linked Tasks in
Nonmodern Societies

The place to begin looking for clues about the origin of sex roles is in the cross-cultural evidence about the division of tasks in nonliterate societies. The task component of roles is the more fundamental of the two components: the task components make up the social organization of societies, while the attribute components merely serve to rationalize that organization. If we find that the cross-cultural data reveal a consistency in the division of labor by sex and if that division of labor is understandable, we will have a valuable insight into how sex roles got started.

In the thirties, anthropologist George Murdock did a cross-cultural analysis of 224 nonliterate societies to find out whether early forms of society divided up tasks between women and men in regular ways.[2] Later Roy D'Andrade reorganized these data and presented them in the form in which they are reproduced here (tables 3.1 and 3.2).

Murdock's data show that although the division of labor by sex is not perfectly consistent throughout these nonliterate societies, certain tasks are predominantly assigned to males while others tend to be assigned to females. Males are usually responsible for duties like hunting, trapping, working with metals, making weapons, and building boats, while females are generally assigned such duties as cooking, carrying water, grinding grain, making pottery, weaving, and making and repairing clothing. The data also show that certain activities are performed by either sex; among these are agriculture and the making of ornaments.

Since very few customs are consistent across societies, whenever such a consistency is found one immediately wonders whether it is biologically determined. That question has of course been asked about the pattern in the division of labor by sex that Murdock first documented. Anthropologists writing in this area are fairly well agreed that although the biological differences between women and men do not directly decree that men must be hunters and women must rear children and do the household chores of cooking and carrying water, certainly the biological differences between the sexes do at least make this division of labor understandable.

Anthropologists since Murdock have pointed to three basic biological differences between men and women to account for the division of labor by sex in nonmodern

3.1/CROSS-CULTURAL DATA FROM 224 SOCIETIES ON SUBSISTENCE ACTIVITIES AND DIVISION OF LABOR BY SEX

Activity	NUMBER OF SOCIETIES IN WHICH ACTIVITY IS PERFORMED BY:				
	Men always	Men usually	Either sex	Women usually	Women always
Pursuit of sea mammals	34	1	0	0	0
Hunting	166	13	0	0	0
Trapping small animals	128	13	4	1	2
Herding	38	8	4	0	5
Fishing	98	34	19	3	4
Clearing land for agriculture	73	22	17	5	13
Dairy operations	17	4	3	1	13
Preparing and planting soil	31	23	33	20	37
Erecting and dismantling shelter	14	2	5	6	22
Tending fowl and small animals	21	4	8	1	39
Tending and harvesting crops	10	15	35	39	44
Gathering shellfish	9	4	8	7	25
Making and tending fires	18	6	25	22	62
Bearing burdens	12	6	35	20	57
Preparing drinks and narcotics	20	1	13	8	57
Gathering fruits, berries, nuts	12	3	15	13	63
Gathering fuel	22	1	10	19	89
Preservation of meat and fish	8	2	10	14	74
Gathering herbs, roots, seeds	8	1	11	7	74
Cooking	5	1	9	28	158
Carrying water	7	0	5	7	119
Grinding grain	2	4	5	13	114

SOURCE: Roy G. D'Andrade, "Sex Differences and Cultural Institutions," in The Development of Sex Differences, ed. Eleanor E. Maccoby, (Stanford: Stanford University Press, 1966), p. 177.

3.2/CROSS-CULTURAL DATA ON THE MANUFACTURE OF OBJECTS AND DIVISION OF LABOR BY SEX

Activity	NUMBER OF SOCIETIES IN WHICH ACTIVITY IS PERFORMED BY:				
	Men always	Men usually	Either sex	Women usually	Women always
Metalworking	78	0	0	0	0
Weaponmaking	121	1	0	0	0
Boat building	91	4	4	0	1
Manufacture of musical instruments	45	2	0	0	1
Work in wood and bark	113	9	5	1	1
Work in stone	68	3	2	0	2
Work in bone, horn, shell	67	4	3	0	3
Manufacture of ceremonial objects	37	1	13	0	1
House building	86	32	25	3	14
Net making	44	6	4	2	11
Manufacture of ornaments	24	3	40	6	18
Manufacture of leather products	29	3	9	3	32
Hide preparation	31	2	4	4	49
Manufacture of nontextile fabrics	14	0	9	2	32
Manufacture of thread and cordage	23	2	11	10	73
Basketmaking	25	3	10	6	82
Mat making	16	2	6	4	61
Weaving	19	2	2	6	67
Pottery making	13	2	6	8	77
Manufacture and repair of clothing	12	3	8	9	95

SOURCE: Roy D'Andrade, "Sex Differences and Cultural Institutions," in The Development of Sex Differences, ed. Eleanor E. Maccoby (Stanford: Stanford University Press, 1966), p. 178.

societies.[3] These are: men are physically stronger, only women get pregnant, and only women can breastfeed children. Let us consider the impact of these differences on the division of tasks by sex in what anthropologists consider to be the earliest form of human society: the hunting and gathering society.

In this type of society, the people subsisted through some combination of hunting wild animals, fishing, and gathering fruits and vegetables from the natural environment.[4] Hunters relied primarily on spears, bows and arrows, and sometimes nets to trap animals. Therefore physical strength was important. How fast the hunter could run or how far he could throw a spear might well determine whether or not he was able to get enough food for his family. Since, as we noted in the previous chapter, there is a biological basis for men's greater physical strength, it is not surprising that Murdock's data show that hunting was done almost exclusively by men in nonliterate societies.

The fact that women bear children also limits the way tasks can be divided in hunting and gathering societies. A woman seven or eight months pregnant would certainly have problems hunting antelope on foot assisted by only a spear or a bow and arrow. And, of course, life expectancy was not seventy-five years for American women as it now is in American society; instead, demographers estimate it was under thirty.[5] Furthermore, infant and child mortality rates were very high. So instead of having two pregnancies between puberty and age seventy-five, as the average woman today does, women in early hunting and gathering societies had many more pregnancies during a lifetime that was probably at least forty-five years shorter. The average woman in a hunting and gathering society spent practically all her adult life either pregnant or with small children about. It is understandable, then, that she usually was not sent out on tasks like hunting or warfare but stayed at home doing such tasks as cooking, weaving, and making pottery and clothing.

The fact of pregnancy also throws some light on the question why men rather than women inevitably held the positions of authority in nonmodern societies.[6] Religious, governmental, or military leadership requires either constant attention or immediate attention at unexpected times, or perhaps both. It would have been very difficult for women to function in these roles, being pregnant so much of their adult lives and having small children to care for. What's more, the major form of nourishment for infants and young children in these societies was mother's milk. This meant that women were limited to those tasks that would allow them to be near their young children.

The God-created reproductive differences between men and women are sufficient to explain the regularities in the division of tasks by sex that Murdock's data show. As he states, "It is unnecessary to invoke innate psychological differences to account for the division of labor by sex; the indisputable differences in reproductive functions suffice to lay out the broad lines of cleavage."[7]

The fact that women bear and nurse children continued to have a significant impact on the division of tasks by sex throughout all forms of nonmodern societies. Even in the preindustrial agricultural societies of a century and a half ago, birth and death rates were comparatively high, women nursed their children, and life expectancy was only in the early forties.[8] Throughout nearly all of human history, then, women have been significantly limited in the societal tasks they could perform by their reproductive functions of pregnancy and nursing.

What we have said about Murdock's data should not be hastily interpreted to mean that men have inevitably played the provider role in nonmodern societies while women have made little contribution to this task. As Judith Brown has noted, it is not that women do not take part in providing subsistence for the family in nonmodern societies but rather that their subsistence activities must be consonant with child-care responsibilities. She writes:

> Women are most likely to make a substantial contribution when subsistence activities have the following characteristics: the participant is not obliged to be far from home; the tasks are relatively monotonous and do not require rapt concentration; and the work is not dangerous, can be performed in spite of interruptions, and is easily resumed once interrupted.[9]

Brown's analysis throws additional light on Murdock's data. Some subsistence activities (e.g., hunting, trapping) are performed almost exclusively by men, while others (e.g., gathering food and fuel, agriculture) are done by either sex. Hunting and trapping are often dangerous and usually require traveling considerable distances from home, and so it would be unlikely that women, with their nursing and other child-care responsibilities, would be assigned to these tasks. They can, however, take part in other subsistence activities, such as gathering and agriculture.

A long-standing assumption in anthropology and sociology has been that males were the primary providers for the family in practically all societies. Recently two researchers, Aronoff and Crano, did a cross-cultural study of 862 societies using data from Murdock's *World Ethnographic Atlas*.[10] Their purpose was to determine the extent to which men and women performed the providing function for the family. The researchers paid attention to the contributions of the sexes to each subsistence activity in every society, as well as to the relative contribution of each subsistence activity to the total subsistence of the society. Their general conclusion was that in the 862 societies they studied, women contributed an average of 44 percent of the subsistence.

Aronoff and Crano's study suggests that women tend to play the provider role almost to the extent that men do in most societies. This was also true of American society as long as it was agrarian. Both women and men worked the family farm. In fact, not until American society became heavily urbanized and industrialized were women removed from the "provider" role. Only then did the care of children and the home come to be considered a full-time task for women.

In summary, the origin and perpetuation of sex roles in nonmodern societies may be found in the fact that God created two biologically distinct sets of human beings. In nonmodern societies, the reproduction differences between women and men clearly set limits on the tasks they could effectively accomplish.

At the same time we must realize that practically any task generally assigned to one sex can at the same time be found to be partially the task of the other sex in at least one society.[11] Males are usually responsible for warfare the world over, but Polynesian, Dahoman, Israeli, and Russian women have all been engaged in combat at some time with cultural sanction. Males generally hold the positions of authority in society, but queens and other female leaders with significant power are scattered throughout history. Women characteristically clean and tend babies, but among the Pygmies of Africa men are as likely to do this as women when the men are in camp.[12] That reproductive differences set only limits on the divison of labor by sex and that there are always exceptions to the pattern was fully documented three decades ago by Margaret Mead in her book *Male and Female*.[13] The only duties that are without exception performed by only one sex, says Mead, are childbearing and nursing.

*A Note on Sex-Role Attributes
in Nonmodern Societies*

In this chapter we have argued that the origin and persistence of sex roles in nonmodern societies is attributable to the reproductive differences between men and women. Other explanations have been offered. Some, for instance, find the source of sex roles in supposed differences in temperament. Steven Goldberg, for one, argues that men are innately more aggressive than women to such an extent that they will always play a dominant, provider-protector role in human society.[14] In the previous chapter of this book we reviewed evidence that suggests there is not a firm biological basis for significant differences in temperament between the sexes. There are also cross-cultural data indicating that it is incorrect to find the origin of sex roles in universal male and female temperaments.

Anthropologist Margaret Mead, who has done numerous cross-cultural studies, argues that much of human behavior results from the influence of culture instead of from innate predispositions. After analyzing the behavior of women and men among the Arapesh, Mundugumor, and Tchambuli of New Guinea, she came to the same conclusion about sex and temperament. Of the three tribes she writes:

> In one, both men and women act as we expect women to act—in a mild parental responsive way; in the second, both act as we expect men to act—in a fierce initiating fashion; and in the third, the men act according to our stereotype for women—are catty, wear curls, and go shopping, while the women are energetic, managerial, unadorned partners.[15]

If the temperaments of men and women can vary so much among three societies living no more than a hundred miles apart, it is highly doubtful that innate psychological differences between women and men are the basis of sex roles. If there are such differences in temperament, in a number of societies they have not been strong enough to withstand cultural influences.

Application to Modern Society

The argument of this chapter has been that there is a biological basis for the origin and perpetuation of sex roles in nonmodern societies. Only women can get pregnant, only women can nurse children, and men are physically stronger: these facts do much to account for the way labor has been divided throughout history. But do these three biological differences have the same implications in modern society?

In a hunting society, one's livelihood often depended on physical strength. That rarely holds true in modern societies. With the Industrial Revolution, mankind learned how to harness inanimate sources of power (oil, electricity, nuclear power); today, one analyst estimates, 90 percent of the work formerly done by animal or human muscle power is accomplished by machines.[16] Physical strength no longer has the importance for the provider role that it once had. The prestigious and well-paying occupations in modern society generally require not physical strength but rather qualities like intelligence and high motivation. One need not have well-developed muscles to be a successful surgeon, attorney, or business executive.

Nor do pregnancy and nursing limit the types of work women can do to the extent that they did in preindustrial societies. With increased life expectancy, changed opinions about ideal family size, and the availability of effective contraceptive devices, women no longer spend the major share of their adult lives pregnant or with small children. And with the discovery of germ control through sterilization, bottle feeding of infants became a relatively safe alternative to breast feeding.

Since the biological basis of sex roles in nonmodern societies is no longer applicable in present-day industrial societies, and since the alternative biological explanation for sex roles in modern societies considered in chapter 2 is not supported by the research evidence, we must turn to something other than biology to account for the content of sex roles in modern society.

Discussion Questions

1/ Discuss the role expectations that are attached to the status of "college student." What tasks are included in this set of expectations? Has society developed a set of attributes in connection with this status? If so, what are these attributes?

2/ In view of what we have noted in this chapter about changes in the anthropological and sociological factors affecting the division of tasks between the sexes, do you think sex roles will disappear in the future? Why or why not?

3/ Was there a pattern in the division of tasks between men and women in biblical times? If so, how would you account for this pattern?

Suggested Readings

Bierstedt, Robert. **The Social Order.** New York: McGraw-Hill Book Co., 1974.

Two chapters are especially helpful in the present context. Chapter 9 contains a fairly extensive treatment of the sociological notions of status and role. Chapter 14 offers an amusing, yet insightful treatment of how biological and social factors contributed to the development of sex roles.

Brown, Judith K. **"A Note on the Divison of Labor by Sex."** *American Anthropologist* 72 (1970), pp. 1073-78.

A succinct statement of the factors influencing the extent to which women will participate in subsistence activities in any given society.

D'Andrade, Roy G. **"Sex Differences and Cultural Institutions."** In *The Development of Sex Differences,* edited by Eleanor E. Maccoby, pp. 174-204. Stanford: Stanford University Press, 1966.

By examining cross-cultural data, D'Andrade develops the thesis that the foundation of sex roles in human societies may be found in a division of tasks that is directly influenced by the reproductive differences between the sexes. Once the division of labor is established, society expands sex roles by sex-linking additional tasks that are in some ways similar to those tasks in the initial division of labor by sex; these additional tasks, however, are only incidentally related to reproductive and strength differences between women and men.

Mead, Margaret. **Sex and Temperament in Three Primitive Societies.** New York: Mentor Books, 1950.

This anthropological classic explodes the myth that sex roles originated in innate psychological differences between the sexes. Three tribes living in the same region are found to have widely differing notions of masculinity and femininity.

/4/

SOCIAL INFLUENCES TOWARD TRADI-TIONAL SEX ROLES

Since only vestiges of a biological basis for sex roles remain in modern American society, the source of the continued existence of these roles must be found primarily in present-day patterns of socialization. Socialization may be defined as "the training people are given in order for them to learn what their statuses are and how to perform the roles attached to those statuses."[1] By learning various status-role combinations through the socialization process, a person develops an identity as well as the motivations and knowledge he or she must have to behave acceptably in society.[2]

The process of socialization begins soon after birth and continues until death. In this lifelong process persons are taught their statuses and roles through such agents as the family, peer group, school, church, and mass media. To a certain extent, the socialization process is unique for each person, depending on his or her individual experiences. However, overall cultural patterns of socialization can be recognized, and these account for the sizable agreement in role definitions and behaviors observable in the majority of people in a society.[3]

Although traditional sex roles are becoming blurred in American society, there are still many social influences toward traditional female and male tasks and attributes. In this chapter we will examine some of these influences.

Preschool Socialization

Almost at the moment the announcement "It's a boy" or "It's a girl" is made, sex-role socialization begins. Baby girls are wrapped in pink blankets, boys in blue ones. Adults speak to and handle boy babies and girl babies differently. Analysts have found variations in the behavior of girl and boy babies at very young ages, and in many cases these differences have been linked to differences in treatment by the parents.

Researchers Goldberg and Lewis observed mothers with their thirteen-month-old infants and found that girl infants touched and talked to their mothers more and remained closer to them than boy infants.[4] This tendency of the girls to show more "dependence" and less "exploratory" behavior was traceable to the way their mothers had treated them earlier. The same babies and mothers had been observed when the infants were six months old. At that time the mothers of girl babies touched, talked to, and handled their infants more than the mothers of boy babies.

To find out whether there was a direct link between the mothers' socialization practice (frequency of touching) and the infants' behavior (the degree to which they sought contact with their mothers), Goldberg and Lewis divided the mothers into three groups according to how much they touched their babies: high, medium, and low. The researchers discovered that the more the mothers touched their six-month-old infants, the more the infants sought contact with their mothers later on. This finding held for both girls and boys.[5]

This research is significant because it shows that sex-role socialization begins very early—long before children have developed any idea of what sex they are. As Lenore Weitzman, an expert on sex-role socialization, says:

> Cultural assumptions about what is "natural" for a boy or for a girl are so deeply ingrained that parents may treat their children differentially without even being aware of it. Presumably, if we interviewed mothers of six-month-old babies, they would not tell us that they expected their sons to be independent and assertive while still in the cradle. Yet it appears that at some level mothers do have such expectations, and these expectations are successfully communicated to very young babies.[6]

Research evidence indicates that three-year-old children are not fully aware of sex differences, nor do they have clear-cut notions of what behavior is appropriate for their sex.[7] The fourth and fifth years are a period of sex-role clarification, and by their sixth year most children are clear about what sex they belong to and how persons of that sex are expected to conduct themselves. How do they learn these roles in so short a time?

Much sex-role learning in the preschool years is likely to occur through simple observation. A child usually sees his father leave the house each weekday to go to work, while his mother stays home and cares for him and the rest of the household. Other adults that he encounters are likely to follow the same pattern. His parents and other adults serve as role models for the child; their behavior gives him an idea of what he might expect in the future.

Another thing that influences very young children to learn sex-appropriate tasks is the toys they are given.[8] The boy who receives a toy cement mixer, soldier set, or doctor kit for Christmas is being taught somthing about sex-linked activities, as is the girl who is given a tea set or sewing kit. Although this cultural pattern may be receding somewhat, a boy is still unlikely to be given a doll or a girl a dump truck because of our preconceived role patterns.

Picture books are another important socialization influence on young children.[9] These books are one of the child's first sources of information about what happens outside her or his own home. Research by Weitzman and associates on prize-winning picture books shows that the books stereotype the attributes and tasks of both sexes.[10] Boys are portrayed as active; they are engaged in adventuresome activities like diving, swimming, racing, hiking, and climbing. Girls are represented as passive, pretty creatures; often they are shown just watching the more exciting activities of the boys. Boys are usually pictured outdoors, where they lead and engage in activities requiring independence and self-confidence, such as rescuing girls and helpless animals. Picture-book girls are more often found indoors, where they work at traditional female tasks such as helping to serve meals to their fathers and brothers.

According to Weitzman and her colleagues, preschool picture books also stereotype the characteristics and activities of adult men and women.[11] Men are storekeepers, kings, fighters, policemen, adventurers, fathers, preachers, judges, and farmers. Women are mothers and wives. The relationship of parents to children is also stereotyped: fathers introduce children to the exciting things in the outside world while mothers serve their children. Weitzman and her colleagues characterize the books' stereotypes of parents in this way:

> Daddies take you on trips in cars, buses, and trains; Daddies take you to the circus, park, and zoo; buy you ice cream; and teach you to swim. Daddies also understand you better because they "know you're big enough and brave enough to do lots of things that mommies think are much too hard for you." Mothers, however, are useful for taking care of you when you are sick, cleaning up after you, and telling you what to do.[12]

The adult role models presented in these picture books for preschoolers are obviously unrealistic. Women are wives and mothers, but they also engage in community activities outside the home, and nearly half of them are employed. And while men sometimes do have exciting occupations and take their children on interesting outings, they also help out with the mundane chores of child care, cleaning, dishwashing, and shopping.

Another medium through which preschoolers are exposed to the outside world is television. Although no complete analysis of children's programming and sex-role socialization has been done, there is evidence that even the more progressive children's programs are not yet fully sensitive to sex-role stereotyping. Gardner found traditional conceptions of male and female roles strongly portrayed in the television program "Sesame Street":

> On one program, Big Bird (having said that he would like to be a member of a family and having been told that Gordon and Susan would be his family) is told that he will have to do men's work—the heavy work, the important work and also that he should get a girl (bird) to help Susan with her work arranging flowers, redecorating, etc. There was more and virtually all of it emphasized that there is men's work and then there is women's work—the men's work is outside the home and women's work is in the home.[13]

Some preschoolers go to day nurseries before they begin to attend school. These nurseries may also influence preschoolers toward traditional sex roles, even when attempts are made to counter such influences. Carole Joffe investigated a nursery school that made a concerted effort to avoid traditional sex-role socialization.[14] All programs and activities in the school were equally available to both sexes. School personnel strongly encouraged both boys and girls to engage in traditionally sex-typed tasks like cooking and washing dishes. The children were permitted to use the same bathroom. The desire to avoid customary socialization practices went so far as to show tolerance toward behavior considered appropriate only for the opposite sex—for example, dressing them. Despite these efforts to avoid typical sex-role socialization, such training still occurred in subtle ways. Boys were more frequently complimented for being able to take care of themselves physically like "little men," while girls were more commonly admired for their pretty clothes and general appearance. The stories read, the games played, and the songs taught stereotyped the attributes and activities of both sexes. Moreover, all the adults at the nursery school were women, which suggested to the children that the care of small children is exclusively the task of adult females while men are busy at other activities.

Although analysts do not fully agree on the precise importance of each of these early socialization influences or on the exact process by which children come to distinguish and internalize male and female roles,[15] it is evident that these early influences are effective. By the time children reach school they can distinguish "feminine" and "masculine" attributes and activities in line with general cultural expectations.[16]

Childhood and Adolescent Socialization

When children reach the age of five or six, they become exposed to a wider range of socialization agents. Among these is the school. Various activities surrounding the school serve to reinforce patterns of preschool sex-role socialization and hence continue societal pressure toward traditional male and female roles.

One of the many ways in which children learn cultural values is through the stories they read, and so Child, Potter, and Levine examined third-grade readers published since 1930.[17] Females and their activities are apparently less worthy of attention, the researchers found, since 73 percent of the central characters in these third-grade readers are male and only 27 percent are female. The sex ratio is similar for secondary characters: 63 percent male, 37 percent female. In addition to suggesting to their readers that females are less important, these stories present the same stereotyped image of females that is characteristic of preschool picture books. As Child and his colleagues put it:

> Female characters . . . are relatively more frequent among those displaying affiliation, nurturance, and harm avoidance. On the other hand, females are less frequent, relatively, among characters displaying activity, aggression, achievement, and recognition. Girls and women are thus being shown as sociable, kind and timid, but inactive, unambitious and uncreative.[18]

This study was conducted a number of years ago. More recent studies, however, find essentially the same pattern. For instance, Marten and Matlin analyzed the illustrations and story content of reading textbooks from a wide range of publishers at both the first- and sixth-grade levels.[19] Their study showed that only 23 percent of the human main characters were female and, further, that while males were five times as likely to be represented in active as opposed to passive behavior, females were portrayed passively as often as actively. Their analysis also indicated that rigidly stereotyped images of women's tasks and attributes are still being presented in elementary readers. According to Marten and Matlin, the latest editions of these readers contain comments like " 'it's girls' work to do dishes,' and 'a woman's place is in the kitchen among the pots and pans.' Furthermore, one edition showed a cartoon of a woman in a driving school with her (male) instructor, and she had accidentally driven the car into a pond. The caption read 'If I had wanted the car washed, I would have said so!' "[20]

The content of elementary-school readers is very important, since reading is perhaps the most basic skill the elementary school attempts to teach and hence a good deal of time is spent with reading textbooks. Yet the school can influence students toward traditional conceptions of sex roles in other ways as well. Saario and colleagues studied the test batteries from each of the major test-publishing companies.[21] Their content analysis turned up the same patterns of sex-role stereotyping that exist in elementary readers. Women were portrayed almost exclusively in household tasks or hobbies. Boys were shown in active roles like camping, hiking, and climbing. Boys exhibited the qualities of responsibility and leadership; girls helped out with the chores at home. The tests also suggested to their young readers that certain occupations belong to one sex or the other. For example, teachers were almost always presented as women, while the doctors were always men.

The school's rigid portrayal of nonoverlapping sex roles is reflected in the way many young children perceive the attributes and tasks of the sexes. For example, Ruth Hartley interviewed boys eight to eleven years old to find out how they viewed male and female roles.[22] Her subjects told her what the masculine role requires of young boys:

> They have to be able to fight in case a bully comes along; they have to be athletic; they have to be able to run fast; they must be able to play rough games; they need to know how to play many games—curb-ball, baseball, basketball, football; they need to be smart; they need to be able to take care of themselves; they should know what girls don't know—how to climb, how to make a fire, how to carry things; they should have more ability than girls; they need to know how to stay out of trouble; they need to know arithmetic and spelling more than girls do.[23]

These same young boys characterized the nature and activities of young girls in this way:

> They have to stay close to the house; they are expected to play quietly and be gentler than boys; they are often afraid; they must

not be rough; they have to keep clean; they cry when they are scared or hurt; they are afraid to go to rough places like rooftops and empty lots; their activities consist of "fopperies," like playing with dolls, fussing over babies, and sitting and talking about dresses; they need to know how to cook, sew, and take care of children, but spelling and arithmetic are not as important for them as for boys.[24]

Hartley also asked the boys about their images of adult men and women. This is what they thought about men:

They need to be strong; they have to be ready to make decisions; they must be able to protect women and children in emergencies; they have to have more manual strength than women; they should know how to carry heavy things; they are the ones to do the hard labor, the rough work, the dirty work, and the unpleasant work; they must be able to fix things; they must get money to support their families; they need "a good business head." . . . In the family, they are the boss; they have authority in relation to the disposal of monies and they get first choice in the use of the most comfortable chair in the house and the daily paper.[25]

In contrast to this image of adult men as strong and active, adult women were perceived as passive, weak, and unintelligent:

They are indecisive; they are afraid of many things; they make a fuss over things; they get tired a lot; they very often need someone to help them; they stay home most of the time; they are not as strong as men; they don't like adventure; they are squeamish about seeing blood; they don't know what to do in an emergency; they cannot do dangerous things; they are more easily damaged than men; and they die more easily than men. Moreover, they are "lofty" about dirty jobs; they feel themselves above manual work; they are scared of getting wet or getting an electric shock; they cannot do things men do because they have a way of doing things the wrong way; they are not very intelligent; they can only scream in an emergency where a man would take charge. Women are the ones who have to keep things neat and tidy and clean up household messes.[26]

As youngsters move into adolescence, the school continues to socialize them into aspects of traditional sex roles. Historically, teachers and counselors have often encouraged girls to take home economics and secretarial-skill courses while boys have more frequently been nudged toward mathematics and science. Saario and colleagues document how in vocational education adolescent girls have been consistently tracked into consumer, homemaking, and health courses while boys are channeled into technical courses like metallurgy, engineering, and police science.[27]

The athletic curriculum of the high school also has encouraged traditional conceptions of masculinity and femininity by continuing a pattern that starts much earlier in most places. Just as communities have for years supported Little League baseball and football teams for boys but not for girls, high schools in the past have allocated more time, money, personnel, and physical facilities to boys' than to girls' sports programs.[28] The socialization message is clear: the school expects the girls to be spectators and cheerleaders while boys participate in athletics and hence develop their physical skills. The conception of males as more active and females as more passive is again reinforced.

A very influential socializing agency during late childhood and adolescence is the peer group, which is a group in which persons of the same age and social status interact. According to sociologists, the adolescent peer group frequently socializes its members into attitudes and values that are at odds with those that parents and teachers are trying to instill. Interestingly, this conflicting socialization does not seem to be present in the matter of sex roles.

James Coleman studied students from a broad range of high schools.[29] These adolescents were questioned about what it takes for boys and girls to be popular among their peers. The answers: Athletic success and leadership in various activities play a major role in making a boy popular. For girls, popularity involves not so much individual achievement as becoming a desirable object to boys. Girls should be physically attractive, have an appealing manner, and wear "nice" clothes. Or as some of Coleman's adolescent female respondents expressed it, being in the leading crowd had these requirements:

> Wear just the right things, nice hair, good grooming, and have a wholesome personality. . . .
> Have a pleasant personality, good manners, dress nicely, be clean, don't swear, be loads of fun.
> A nice personality, dress nice without overdoing it.
> Hang out at _____'s. Don't be too smart. Flirt with boys. Be cooperative on dates.[30]

One of these answers suggests that something else besides physical attractiveness and a good personality is required for the adolescent girl to be acceptable to boys: "Don't be too smart." As a number of writers have pointed out, being "too smart" means revealing an intelligence comparable or superior to that of male counterparts.[31] This jeopardizes the adolescent girl's popularity by threatening the precarious ego of the adolescent boy.[32]

The adolescent subculture's theme of defining feminine success in terms of attractiveness to men is strongly reinforced by the mass media.[33] Magazines for teen-age girls like *Seventeen* and *Glamour* are guides to success with males. They offer instructions on how to look and act in order to attract the all-important boy. Very little space is devoted to positive portrayals of career women.

Like the school and the peer group, the family also socializes girls and boys toward traditional sex roles. Aberle and Naegele studied a group of middle-class fathers to learn their preferences for the future activities of their sons and daughters.[34] These fathers, without exception, wanted their sons to go to college, and they expected them to go into business or the professions. Most of the fathers also wanted their daughters to have a college education but did not feel it was as necessary for their future as it was for the sons'. And although more than half of these men accepted the possibility that their daughters might have a career, the majority still preferred that the girls marry and establish a family, while a significant minority rejected the idea of a career for their daughters altogether.

Aberle and Naegele also obtained information on the behavior that these fathers valued in their sons and daughters. Fathers were pleased if their sons showed initiative, accepted responsibility, performed well in school, did well athletically, and showed emotional stability. They wanted their daughters, by contrast, to be "'nice,' 'sweet'; pretty, affectionate, and well-liked."[35] Aberle and Naegele explain the difference in the middle-class father's attitudes toward his son's and his daughter's behavior in terms of the different futures he desires for them:

> The ideal-typical successful adult male in the middle-class occupational role should be responsible, show initiative, be competent, be aggressive, be capable of meeting competition. . . . He [the father] worries about failures in these areas and is happy over successes, because of his future expectations for his sons. He does not worry so much about his daughters because they will occupy different roles, toward which he has a somewhat vaguer orientation. Occupational career is not taken seriously, marriage is the primary hope and expectation, the same sorts of demands are not made, and the father does not seem to fuss too much as to whether his young daughter will ultimately be a good mate. If she is a sweet little girl, this is enough.[36]

Additional data on both mothers and fathers from a wider range of social-class backgrounds essentially support the study of Aberle and Naegele. Researchers Sewell and Shah studied parental encouragement in relation to the educational aspirations of high school seniors.[37] They found that boys received more encouragement to go on to college than girls did. Since higher education is perceived to be the main route to the "better jobs" and these jobs are a more financially secure way of providing for a family, the fact that parents encourage boys more than girls to go to college may be interpreted as socialization toward traditional sex roles. The family is telling adolescents that it is more important for boys than girls to prepare themselves for the role of family provider.

In childhood and adolescence, then, a number of agencies of socialization influence youngsters toward traditional sex-role attributes and tasks. The school, peer group, media, and family collectively indicate to young people that females tend to be more affiliative, nurturant, physically inactive, weak, uncreative, and emotional, and males are more independent, aggressive, athletic, strong, creative, and rational. Girls are told to make themselves pretty and appealing to boys; boys are encouraged to achieve as athletes and student leaders. These same agencies also instruct youngsters about what tasks will be foremost for them in the future. Girls can expect to be child rearers and housewives while boys can anticipate being the main family breadwinners.

Continuing Socialization

By late adolescence, a young person is quite clear on societal preferences for most of his or her adult roles. However, cultural influences toward traditional sex roles continue on into adulthood.

One such influence is exercised by certain large-circulation magazines aimed specifically at either women or men. Women's magazines, though they do not present as stereotyped a version of the adult activities of American women as the preschool picture books or school textbooks discussed earlier, still reinforce the traditional female role. For instance, researcher Lovelle Ray sampled issues of *McCall's, Ladies' Home Journal,* and *Cosmopolitan* published from 1965 to 1970.[38] In studying the fictional role models presented in *McCall's* and the *Journal,* she found both housewives and working women represented. However, most of the working women were single and on the lookout for a husband, which suggests that marriage is more fundamental to the adult female role than being single and having a career. In analyzing issues of *Cosmopolitan*, Ray found that the magazine reinforces the dominant theme found in adolescent female socialization: females must concern themselves with attracting a male. Much of the fictional and nonfictional content of *Cosmopolitan* deals with working women, but the emphasis is on attracting men in this arena, not on building careers. This finding is hardly surprising in view of the philosophy of *Cosmopolitan*'s editor, Helen Gurley Brown. As Ray quotes her: "A woman can't have a really wonderful life if she doesn't have a man to go to bed with. We try to tell her how to find her man, how to attract him, to keep him interested, and how to get him back after he has wandered off the reservation."[39]

An even more detailed study of *McCall's, Ladies' Home Journal,* and *Good Housekeeping* reveals that the traditional female role is much more sympathetically portrayed in women's magazines than are alternative roles for women. Margaret Lefkowitz studied the characteristics of the female main characters in the fiction that appeared in these magazines in 1957 and 1967.[40] In both years she found the predominant female role model to be an attractive young married woman whose main activity was housekeeping and whose main goals revolved around romantic love. Other female heroines such as career women were presented for the sake of contrast, but they appeared much less often (in 1967 only 4 percent of female main characters were career women) and were portrayed much less sympathetically. Lefkowitz states that career women "were usually pictured as 'unwomanly' and were seen most often in the act of threatening some 'true' woman's marriage."[41] This positive rein-

forcement of the traditional female role became even
more decided in the later year. By 1967 fewer alternative
role models for women were being presented, and the
housewife-heroines' marriages got even happier.

One need hardly comment about the socialization message of men's magazines like *Playboy*. The idealized
male is successful to the point where he can enjoy the
best of consumer items. He is a person who, as Harvey
Cox puts it, always remains "cool and unruffled." [42]
Playboy also projects to its male readers a distinct image
of women. Women are to be beautiful, sexy, and, most
important of all, appealing to men. The centerfold of the
magazine leaves the impression that the young female is
a "playmate," to be related to as the idealized male relates
to other objects in his life. "Sex becomes one of the items
of leisure activity that the knowledgeable consumer of
leisure handles with his characteristic skill and detach-
ment," Cox comments. "The girl becomes a desirable—
indeed an indispensable—'Playboy accessory.' " [43]

Advertising is another social influence on adults that
fosters traditional, stereotypical conceptions of women's
and men's roles. [44] Judging from the products that American advertising aims at women, they have only two primary tasks in adulthood: making themselves glamourous
for men and caring for the household. The advertisements most often directed at women are for cosmetics,
fashions, soaps, detergents, polishes, child-care products,
and foods. [45] Advertisements for business machines,
tools, and lawn mowers make it quite clear that men play
the family breadwinner role along with doing some maintenance tasks around the house on weekends.

The advertising world also projects a stereotypical
image of the attributes of men and women. The strong,
rugged individualist of the Marlboro ads is male. Those
driving cars fast or over rugged terrain are more often
male. The person usually offering—and thus presumably

capable of giving—advice in TV commercials is male. In contrast, women are frequently stereotyped as sex objects. The provocatively clad woman is used to sell not only panty hose but also automobile shock absorbers, cigars, and shaving cream. Another traditional female role attribute commonly projected by advertising is nurturance. The person giving cough syrup to another member of the family or putting a bandage on a minor wound is usually a woman. Finally, many advertisements about household cleaning products suggest that women are not very intelligent. They are often shown getting unaccountably excited about products that give a "lemon scented" shine to their furniture, a "nonyellowing" radiance to their floors, a "brilliant" whiteness to their laundry, or an "effortless" cleanliness to their ovens. Of particular interest in this connection are the many so-called experiments in TV commercials that are supposed to demonstrate the superiority of one cleaning product over another. The unknowledgeable subjects in the experiments are invariably women, and though, judging from TV commercials, men rarely put their hands in soap suds or do the laundry, still the person intelligent enough to administer the experiment, summarize its results, and indicate to the female subjects which product they ought to buy is almost always a man.

Watching television takes up more of the leisure time of Americans than any other single activity.[46] In a broad analysis of this mass medium, Stanford University developmental psychologist Sharon Churnin Nash found that, like commercials, afternoon "soaps" and prime-time comedies and dramas stereotype the roles of women and men.[47] Her analysis reveals that by and large men and women are shown in very traditional activities and roles. Women are not represented in TV programming in a way that represents the extent of their participation in the labor force. Men are pictured as more rational and independent, whereas women are more often portrayed as overly emotional and in need of advice. Although prime-time programming has by no means rid itself of such traditional images, the afternoon remains the bastion of sex-role stereotyping:

> Afternoon "soaps" foster an ideology based on feminine passivity, ineptness, and subservience. Even independent women of the highest professional stature manage to get themselves in . . . messes from which only strong, brave, intelligent males can extricate them. The soap opera heroines are always acted upon. They are raped, divorced, abandoned, misunderstood, given drugs, and attacked by mysterious diseases.[48]

The state of affairs with popular music is much the same. Kay Reinartz examined a sample of two thousand popular songs published over a ninety-year period beginning with 1880.[49] The men who wrote these songs (90 percent were written by men) have propagated an ideology in which the significance of women lies in three things: the sex, love, and general service they can give to men. In elaborating on these three feminine tasks, popular songs present the female at one of two extremes: either an unreal "angel" who brings the male nothing but happiness or the "embodiment of evil" who is deceitful and brings him sorrow. Reinartz states that the stereotypes of women in popular songs have changed little over the past century. In the 1970s women are still being presented as "deceitful, excessively emotional, sentimental, illogical, frivolous. . . ."[50]

The year 1976 marked the two-hundredth birthday of the United States and the one-hundredth birthday of the telephone. To celebrate both, the Bell System designed covers for its telephone directories that pictured American cultural heroes conversing over both vintage and modern telephones. An analysis of those covers is informative. Twenty-two male cultural heroes are pictured and only seven female cultural heroes—eight if one counts the Statue of Liberty. The types of males and females selected by Bell as cultural heroes are also revealing. The males are such persons as Benjamin Franklin, Thomas Jefferson, John D. Rockefeller, Abraham Lincoln, Frederick Douglass, Norman Rockwell, and Paul Revere. These men were all individual achievers, especially in the areas of politics and economics. Six of the seven female cultural heroes appear to have been picked on another basis. They are: Betsy Ross, a Spanish senorita, a telephone operator, an American teen-ager chattering on the phone, Whistler's mother, and Shirley Temple. Marian Anderson is pictured also, but she seems to have been picked more as a black than as a female, for the caption reads: ". . . the first black artist in the history of the Metropolitan Opera." If the norm of individual achievement had been used to select both female and male cultural heroes, one might have expected to see such women as Margaret Sanger, Frances Perkins, and Amelia Earhart.

Conclusion

The data and arguments considered in the two chapters before this one make it clear that the continued existence of traditional sex roles in modern American society is primarily the result of the socialization process. The biological evidence does not warrant the conclusion that men are better suited for the provider task and women for the child-rearing and household-care tasks. Nor do the biological data suggest significant differences in the innate psychological attributes of the sexes. Much of the biological evidence is confirmed by the cross-cultural observations of anthropologists. Overall in human societies, men and women have contributed almost equally to family provision. Moreover, attributes thought to be female or male in one society have been found to be linked to the opposite sex in another society. In the absence of a satisfactory biological explanation, the persistence of discernible sex roles must be accounted for by social influences.

In this chapter we have looked at a wide range of socialization agencies. The research evidence clearly indicates that these agencies continue to encourage people to behave and think according to the traditional sex roles.

This point must be kept in perspective. No type of socialization is perfectly consistent or totally effective. Every person has some learning experiences that are at odds with the dominant patterns of socialization. For example, Mirra Komarovsky pointed out over two decades ago that in addition to being socialized into traditional patterns of caring for the household, rearing children, being glamourous, and being a wife, American women are increasingly being exposed to social influences toward a "modern role."[51] The newer role for women contains expectations of educational and occupational achievement similar to the expectations in the traditional male role. This inconsistency in the socialization of women is reflected in the media. Although the dominant pattern there reinforces the traditional stereotype of the activities of women, some advertisements, TV programs, and the like serve to break down the stereotype and thus reinforce the "modern" female role of individual achievement in a career.[52]

A second qualification affecting the evidence about sex-role socialization has to do with the complexity of American society. The United States is made up of many diverse socio-economic, ethnic, religious, racial, and marital status groups, and among these groups there are variations in beliefs about the appropriate behaviors of women and men.[53] For example, working-class parents tend to sex-type activities along traditional lines more frequently and consistently than middle-class parents. And no matter what their social class, black girls are encouraged to be more independent than white girls. Such variations are numerous, and so a complete description of sex-role socialization is practically impossible.

On the whole, however, the social influences discussed here seem to reflect the dominant themes of sex-role socialization in American society. Broverman and colleagues, recognizing that traditional roles had come under significant criticism by feminists and others during the past decade, conducted research in the mid-seventies to ascertain whether or not there was still agreement about the roles of men and women and, if so, to what groups in society that agreement extended.[54] They found a strong consensus on the traditional content of female and male roles. They also found that this agreement cut across groups differing in age, sex, religion, marital status, and educational level. Apparently, traditional patterns of sex-role socialization still prevail in American society.

Discussion Questions

1/ The first four chapters of this book make it evident that the author thinks sex roles in modern American society are more deeply rooted in the prevailing socialization practices than in the biological differences between men and women. Do you agree? Do you perceive any distortions here?

2/ Try to describe the ways and extent to which your parents, teachers, ministers, and friends encouraged you to internalize either the traditional female or the traditional male role. Were the socialization practices you experienced fairly consistent with those described in this chapter?

3/ Do you think traditional patterns of sex-role socialization are breaking down? If so, in what ways? Are they receding most obviously in the home, the church, the school, or the mass media?

4/ Do you think children should still be reared according to the traditional sex-role socialization process? Why or why not?

Suggested Readings

Broverman, Inge K., Susan Raymond Vogel, Donald M. Broverman, Frank E. Clarkson, and Paul S. Rosenkrantz. "**Sex-Role Stereotypes: A Current Appraisal.**" In *Women and Achievement: Social and Motivational Analyses,* edited by Martha Tamara Shuch Mednick, Sandra Schwartz Tangri, and Lois Wladis Hoffman, pp. 32-47. New York: John Wiley & sons, 1975.

A report on research designed to find out whether the considerable criticism of traditional sex-role socialization practices during the past decade has affected people's notions of female and male roles. The researchers found that traditional conceptions still prevail.

Goldberg, Susan, and Michael Lewis. **"Play Behavior in the Year-Old Infant: Early Sex Differences."** *Child Development,* March-June 1969, pp. 21-31.

Documents how sex-role socialization begins long before a child has a concept of which sex she or he belongs to. The authors illustrate well the subtlety of certain sex-role socialization practices.

International Reading Association. **The Reading Teacher** 29 (May 1976), pp. 743-93.

A magazine issue devoted entirely to articles on sex differences and reading. A number of the articles report on the socialization message of elementary school readers and tell how the teacher can begin to counteract the sex-role stereotyping found in those books.

Weitz, Shirley. **Sex Roles: Biological, Psychological, and Social Foundations.** New York: Oxford University Press, 1977.

A scholarly and well-documented book that devotes a major section to sex-role socialization from a psychological perspective. Theories of learning, current socialization practices, and the resulting psychological differences between the sexes are reviewed.

/5/

THE SOCIAL COST OF
TRADITIONAL SEX
ROLES

A person's social role limits his opportunities to carry on various activities in society. His role requires him to perform certain social tasks and not others. Then, once he is performing the required tasks, society tries to get him to stay in that role by attributing to him certain characteristics associated with the role.

In the past, the opportunities of black people in American society were severely limited by this basic social process. By attributing to blacks certain characteristics like lack of intelligence, low motivation, natural rhythm, and athletic ability, society did much to limit their opportunities to the more menial societal tasks plus a few positions in the entertainment and sports worlds.

Another important sociological notion about roles is that there are two types: achieved and ascribed.[1] *Achieved* roles are those gained through a person's own

103

accomplishments and choice. Examples are playing defensive tackle for a professional football team, being a physician, being a ditch-digger. *Ascribed* roles are assigned by society at birth on the basis of characteristics over which the person has no control. Examples include racial, ethnic, age, and sex roles. A person can do little about the fact that he is, say, a white Irish fifteen-year-old male, but society still expects him to behave in certain ways by virtue of each of those characteristics.

The Negative Consequences for Women

Socializing females into traditional tasks like household care and child rearing and into traditional attributes such as being nurturant, service oriented, affiliative, physically attractive, dependent, physically inactive, and emotional has significant consequences for women and for society at large.

As they have entered the labor force, women have had to confront the phenomenon of the sex-typing of occupations. Just as society, in the past, relegated blacks to menial occupations by encouraging a particular stereotype of them, so society has also succeeded in limiting women to certain kinds of jobs by fostering an image of their attributes. Only certain jobs are considered appropriate for women.

One manifestation of the sex-typing of occupations is the fact that out of 250 occupations listed by the U.S. Bureau of the Census, just 21 account for more than half of all employed women.[2] By contrast, it requires 65 occupational titles to account for half of the male labor force. Fully one-fourth of the total female labor force is working at just five occupations: secretary, household worker, bookkeeper, elementary school teacher, and waitress. It is interesting to note that most of these occupations require elements of the same nurturant service orientation that is thought integral to the traditional housewife-mother role.

Using U.S. Bureau of the Census data from 1900 and 1960, Valerie Oppenheimer determined the occupations in which 70 percent or more of the workers were female.[3] The resulting list of "female occupations" and the percentage of each that women compose can be found in Table 5.1. In both years, 1900 and 1960, these "women's jobs" accounted for over one-half of employed women.

By including information from 1900 as well as 1960, Oppenheimer was able to look for changes in occupational sex-typing. The data in Table 5.1 indicate that the only significant change over the sixty-year period was that a greater number of occupations had become predominantly female by 1960. Out of the seventeen occupations found to be 70 percent or more female in 1900, fourteen remained so in 1960.

This finding that the sex-typing of jobs has changed little since the turn of the century is supported further by the research of Edward Gross.[4] Gross developed an index to measure what he termed "sexual segregation" in occupations for each year from 1900 through 1960. Sexual segregation was defined as the number of females (or males) who would have to change jobs in order to have the occupational distribution of female workers correspond to that of male workers. Gross found that sexual segregation in the American labor force has changed little since 1900; the index ranged only from a low of 66 percent to a high of 69 percent. This means that for any given year between 1900 and 1960, approximately two-thirds of either women or men would have had to change jobs in order for the occupational distributions of the two sexes to match. Gross highlighted the degree of sexual segregation in the labor force by comparing its magnitude to racial segregation there. Whereas in 1960, 68 percent of women (or men) would have had to change jobs to produce comparable occupational distributions for each, only 47 percent of non-whites (or whites) would have had

5.1/OCCUPATIONS IN WHICH 70 PERCENT OR MORE OF THE WORKERS WERE WOMEN, 1900 AND 1960

Occupation	Percent female	
	1900	1960
Professional and technical workers		
1. Librarians	72	86
2. Nurses	94	86
3. Dancers & dancing teachers	—	77
4. Teachers	75	72
5. Dietitians & nutritionists (a)	—	93
Clerical workers		
1. Library attendants & assistants	80	77
2. Stenographers, typists, & secretaries	72	96
3. Telephone operators	80	96
4. Attendants, physicians' & dentists' offices (a)	—	98
5. Office machine operators	—	74
6. File clerks (a)	—	86
7. Receptionists (a)	—	98
8. Bookkeepers & cashiers (a)	(31)	82
Sale workers		
1. Demonstrators (b)	(66)	92
Operatives		
1. Dressmakers & seamstresses	100	97
2. Milliners	100	91
3. Apparel & accessories operatives	70	74

4. Knitting mill operatives	78	78
5. Textile spinners (b)	(65)	79
6. Misc. fabricated textile products operatives (c)	71	(61)
7. Fruit, nut, & vegetable graders and packers	71	71
8. Laundry & dry cleaning operatives (b)	(61)	72
9. Sewers & stitchers (a)	—	94
10. Paperboard boxes & containers operatives (c)	84	(33)
Private household workers	97	96
Other service workers		
1. Hospital attendants, practical nurses, & midwives	89	81
2. Boarding & lodging housekeepers	83	88
3. Housekeepers & stewards	78	80
4. Attendants, professional & personal services (a)	—	70
5. Chambermaids & maids (a)	—	98
6. Hairdressers & cosmetologists (a)	—	89
7. Waitresses, counter & fountain workers (b)	(40)	84
8. Charwomen & cleaners (b)	84	(68)

SOURCE: Valerie Kincade Oppenheimer, "The Sex-Labelling of Jobs" in Industrial Relations (May 1968).
(a) Not listed separately in 1900
(b) Less than 70 percent female in 1900
(c) Less than 70 percent female in 1960

to do so. Reflecting on these data, Gross commented:

> Those concerned with sexual segregation as a social problem can take small comfort from these figures. They suggest that the movement of women into the labor market has not meant the disappearance of sexual typing in occupation. Rather, the great expansion in female employment has been accomplished through the expansion of occupations that were already heavily female, through the emergence of wholly new occupations (such as that of keypunch operator) which were defined as female from the start, and through females taking over previously male occupations.[5]

Another measurable consequence of society's traditional conception of the role of women is income discrimination against females. Until recently, income discrimination by sex was not recognized as a problem. This was in large part due to the attitude that men rather than women are the appropriate family providers. Since females traditionally have not been perceived as family providers, employers have often had few qualms about paying working women less than men—"after all, aren't they just working for extras?" Now, however, income discrimination by sex has become a major social issue.

The U.S. Department of Labor reports that the 1974 median income of full-time working females was $6,772. This is far less than the $11,835 recorded for males in the same year.[6] Some argue that this large gap exists not primarily because women are being paid less than men for essentially the same work but because women hold less prestigious jobs and have less education and job experience. Research by Levitin and colleagues, however, does not bear out this line of argument.[7] In analyzing data obtained from a national probability sample of workers over sixteen years of age, they found that even after the figures were adjusted for the differences in degree of education, tenure with the employer, tenure of the specific job with that employer, number of hours worked each week, amount of supervisory responsibility, and prestige of the job, female workers still were paid only 58 percent as much as male workers. Similarly qualified women, then, are being paid considerably less for the same work as their male counterparts. In fact, Levitin and her associates state that employers would have to raise employed women's salaries by an average of 71 percent if equally qualified women and men working at the same jobs were to receive equivalent pay.

Evidence of a different sort of income discrimination comes from the courts. The Equal Pay Act of 1963, Title VII of the 1964 Civil Rights Act, and Executive Orders 11246 and 11375 all legislate against sex discrimination in the labor force. It is now illegal to give jobs, grant promotions, and determine pay on the basis of sex. In analyzing various court cases brought under these laws, Falk concludes that in addition to the direct discrimination of unequal pay for equal work, there is indirect income discrimination.[8] This happens when women are unfairly passed over for promotions and are kept in supposedly different but certainly lower-paid job categories than men.

One example of this sort of discrimination comes from the case of *Bowe* v. *Colgate-Palmolive.*[9] Prior to the passage of Title VII, work at this company's Albany, Indiana, plant was divided into men's jobs and women's jobs. Each job category had its own seniority system with the highest pay rate for women equaling only the lowest rate for men. When Title VII made it illegal to distinguish jobs on the basis of sex, the contract between Colgate-Palmolive and the union was altered. The former "women's jobs" became jobs that required the employee to lift no more than thirty-five pounds; these jobs were now available to male as well as female employees. Former "men's jobs" became jobs that might require lifting over thirty-five pounds; these remained open only to men. This alteration still left women with little potential for promotion and with lower pay rates. Several women brought suit under Title VII, charging that both their union and Colgate-Palmolive were continuing to practice sex discrimination. In reversing the decision of a lower court, the Seventh Circuit Court ordered Colgate-Palmolive to permit all workers, regardless of sex, equal opportunity for all jobs for which they were qualified, and to give women the back pay withheld from them because of discrimination since the passage of Title VII.

To date, the most publicized case of income discrimination against women by means of the artificial creation of separate jobs for men and women is the case of the American Telephone and Telegraph Company (AT&T), the largest private employer of women.[10] Late in 1970, the Equal Employment Opportunity Commission (EEOC), which is the enforcement agency of Title VII, filed petitions charging that AT&T systematically discriminated against both minorities and women. After a year-long investigation, 30,000 pages of testimony, and a final report from the EEOC charging that "the Bell monolith is, without doubt, the largest oppressor of women workers in the United States," AT&T was found guilty of discrimination. Although testimony suggested that sex discrimination by itself resulted in a difference of $500 million per year in wages since the time seven years earlier when such discrimination had become illegal, AT&T was ordered to make compensation in the form of only $38 million in back pay and salary increases.

Besides sex-typing of jobs and income discrimination, a third—and probably the most damaging—consequence of the traditional sex-role socialization of females is that women generally have come to think less of their abilities in certain areas than is warranted. Society encourages its members to think of women primarily according to the pattern of housewife-mother-glamour girl and of men as the economic, political, and educational achievers in their role as family provider. By doing this it encourages women to have in some regards unrealistically low self-concepts. The process is similar to that which has been exercised against blacks. Historically, the white majority has directly and indirectly indicated to blacks that society considers them lower than whites in intellect and motivation and therefore less likely to achieve in economic, political, and intellectual areas. Social psychologists point out that many blacks have internalized this negative definition of their abilities and that the resulting low self-concept, coupled with patterns of discrimination, largely accounts for lower levels of black economic, political, and educational achievement.[11]

Evidence of similar negative self-definitions in women comes from the research of Philip Goldberg.[12] Goldberg wanted to find out whether college women would realistically evaluate individual achievement regardless of the sex of the achiever, or whether society's negative definition of women's ability would prejudice their evaluation. He divided female college subjects into two groups and gave each group a set of six professional articles. The subjects were to evaluate the scholarly competence of the authors. In each set, three articles were supposedly written by men and three by women. The only difference between the two sets was in the manipulation of authors' names—an article carrying a male author's name in one set (e.g., "John T. McKay") had a female author's name in the second set (e.g., "Joan T. McKay"). The result, said Goldberg, was this:

> The girls consistently found an article more valuable—and its author more competent—when the article bore a male name. Though the articles themselves were exactly the same, the girls felt that those written by the John T. McKays were definitely more impressive, and reflected more glory on their authors, than did the mediocre offerings of the Joan T. McKays.[13]

Another finding of Goldberg's suggests even more strongly that women have unrealistically low estimations of the abilities of members of their own sex. Recognizing that academic fields have been sex-typed in much the same way as occupations, Goldberg included articles about both "male fields" (city planning and law) and "female fields" (elementary education and dietetics). He hypothesized that the female college subjects would evaluate an article in a traditionally female field more favorably if they thought it had been written by a woman rather than a man. But he found that "even here, women consider themselves inferior to men. Women seem to think that men are better at *everything*—including elementary-school teaching and dietetics!"[14]

Not only do many women apparently believe that they are generally less talented than men in areas outside the confines of the traditional female role, but they are also more likely than men to be uncomfortable with the prospect of significant achievement by members of their own sex. Matina Horner sought to test for achievement-related conflicts in women by giving a group of college women a thematic lead to a story and asking them to complete the story.[15] The thematic cue read: "After first term finals, Anne finds herself at the top of her medical school class." For purposes of comparison, the same research procedures were followed with a group of college men, except that for them the name in the thematic cue was changed from "Anne" to "John." Over 90 percent of the college men responded positively toward the highly successful male, "John." In completing their stories, the male college subjects indicated that John continued to strive, remained confident in his future, and eventually reached his goal of becoming a successful doctor. Achieving this goal helped John achieve other goals, too, such as providing a secure home for his wife and children. The college women, on the other hand, had quite a different response to their thematic lead of "Anne." States Horner:

> In response to the successful female cue 65% of the girls were
> disconcerted, troubled, or confused by the cue. Unusual excel-
> lence in women was clearly associated for them with the loss of
> femininity, social rejection, personal or societal destruction, or
> some combination of the above. Their responses were filled with
> negative consequences . . . righteous indignation, withdrawal
> rather than enhanced striving, concern, or even an inability to
> accept the information presented in the cue. There was a typical
> story, for example, in which Anne deliberately lowers her
> academic standing the next term and does all she subtly can to
> help Carl, whose grades come up. She soon drops out of med-
> school, they marry and Carl goes on in school while she raises
> their family.[16]

Horner's conclusion is that college women, much more
than college men, fear success because they perceive
that such success will have negative consequences for
them.

From a sociological standpoint, then, women—and indeed society as a whole—pay a considerable price for
traditional female sex-role ascription. It has limited the
range of occupations women can enter, the income they
can earn, the promotions they can obtain, the estimations
they have of the abilities of members of their own sex,
and the desire they have for success in areas outside the
confines of the traditional female role.

In reviewing the social consequences of society's traditional conception of women, one cannot help being
struck by certain similarities in the social forces affecting
the lives of blacks and women. Both have been assigned
negative role attributes, have experienced various forms
of discrimination, and have developed unrealistically
low views of their own abilities. Helen Mayer Hacker
recognized the parallels long ago when she argued that
both blacks and women are subordinate classes in American society. Her summary of the specific similarities,
made in 1951, is instructive and is reprinted here in Table
5.2.

5.2/SIMILARITIES IN THE STATUS OF BLACKS AND WOMEN

Blacks	Women
1. HIGH SOCIAL VISIBILITY	
a. Skin color, other "racial" characteristics	a. Secondary sex characteristics
b. Sometimes distinctive dress patterns	b. Distinctive dress
2. ASCRIBED ATTRIBUTES	
a. Inferior intelligence, smaller brain, less convoluted, scarcity of geniuses	a. Ditto
b. Freer instinctual gratifications; more emotional, "primitive," and childlike; imagined sexual prowess envied	b. Irresponsible, inconsistent, emotionally unstable; lack strong superego; women as temptresses
c. Common stereotype "inferior"	c. "Weaker"
3. RATIONALIZATIONS OF STATUS	
a. Thought all right in his place	a. Women's place is in the home
b. Myth of contented Negro	b. Myth of contented woman—"feminine" woman is happy in subordinate role

4. ACCOMMODATING ATTITUDES

a. Supplicatory intonation of voice

b. Deferential manner

c. Concealment of real feelings

d. Outwit "white folks"

e. Careful study of points at which the dominant group is susceptible to influence

f. Fake appeals for directives; show of ignorance

a. Rising inflection, smiles, laughs, downward glances

b. Flattering manner

c. "Feminine wiles"

d. Outwit "men folk"

e. Ditto

f. Appearance of ignorance

5. DISCRIMINATIONS

a. Limitations of education—should fit "place" in society

b. Confined to traditional jobs—barred from supervisory positions

c. Deprived of political importance

d. Social and professional segregation

e. More vulnerable to criticism

a. Ditto

b. Ditto

c. Ditto

d. Ditto

e. E.g., conduct in bars

SOURCE: *Helen Mayer Hacker, "Women as a Minority Group," Social Forces 30 (October 1951), p. 65.*

The Negative Conse-
quences for Men

The chief components of the traditional male role are being an aggressive, competitive family provider and being the "head of the house," that is, the family's main decision maker. Sociologically, it has generally been thought that men are quite fortunate when compared to women. Men, like women, have been limited in that they have been expected to play a certain role. Yet fulfilling the traditional male role does not predetermine the day-to-day activities of men nearly to the extent that fulfilling the traditional female role predetermines the activities of women.

Psychologists Sandra and Darryl Bem have effectively made this point by suggesting that those who doubt it ask themselves this question about two infants, one male and the other female: whose activities twenty-five years hence can be most precisely predicted? Obviously, the answer is: the female's. It is highly probable that in twenty-five years she will be married, have a small child, and be performing the day-to-day duties of child care and other domestic tasks. About the boy infant, it can be said that he will probably be married and be a family provider, but his daily activities cannot be predicted nearly so precisely. The enterprising man potentially has a large number of areas from which to choose in developing his talents while at the same time he is fulfilling his role of family breadwinner. If he has the motivation and the skills, the adult male can be anything from a janitor to a neurosurgeon.

From a sociological perspective, men have also been thought to be more fortunate than women because their traditional role is more highly valued in American society. Being an economic provider and decision maker brings more prestige and other social rewards than performing tasks like child rearing and household care. The common phrase "just a housewife" reflects this lesser evaluation of the traditional female role.

About the only negative consequence for men that sociologists have found in the traditional male role is the pressure associated with being a provider in a highly competitive and status-conscious society. It has been suggested that this pressure may partially account for men's higher rates of suicide, accident, mental breakdown, and heart disease as well as certain other physical ailments. However, whether these conditions are due to the pressures associated with the provider role or to the biological causes discussed in chapter 2 is basically still an unresearched question.

As the current feminist movement developed, it became increasingly clear that the criticisms leveled at the traditional female role had implications for the traditional male role as well. Consequently a number of books have appeared whose purpose is to heighten consciousness about the limitations placed on men by traditional notions of male tasks and masculinity.[17] The dominant theme running through these treatments of the male role is that significant negative consequences result from the narrow socialization message that men are to "seek achievement and suppress emotion." Because of an overemphasis on achievement, it is argued, men are removed from the rearing of their children, may be incapable of adjusting to retirement, and are more vulnerable to the stress associated with filling the positions of power and responsibility in society. Suppressing emotion, these authors maintain, only accentuates the stress and thereby accounts in part for men's higher rates of suicide, accident, mental breakdown, and heart disease. Although decidedly lacking in empirical data, these recent commentaries on the traditional male role raise provocative issues that deserve careful research.

Conclusion

The content of traditional sex roles has placed considerable limitations on people's expression of their individual talents. The abilities necessary to accomplish different sorts of responsibilities tend to vary much more among individual women and individual men than between men as a group and women as a group. Still, modern society continues to influence men and women toward the rather narrowly conceived expectations of the traditional roles. The result is various forms of discrimination by sex and the other negative consequences recorded in this chapter. In the end, the traditional social script for men and women is accountable for a serious waste of individual talents and hence a loss to society at large.

Discussion Questions

1/ Do you think it is fair to compare the social position of women to that of blacks? Are there significant differences between the two positions?

2/ Do you know anyone who has experienced occupational discrimination based on sex? If so, describe the case.

3/ Was or is there any evidence of sexism at your college? If so, in what areas—textbooks, professors, academic or personal counseling, hiring practices?

4/ Have you ever been personally discriminated against because of your sex? In what manner?

5/ Do you feel there is any justification for the patterns of sex discrimination discussed in this chapter? Explain.

Suggested Readings

Freeman, Jo, ed. **Women: A Feminist Perspective.** Palo Alto, California: Mayfield Publishing Co., 1975.

A major section of this book is devoted to patterns of occupational and economic discrimination against women. Other sections contain some interesting articles on women and self-concept.

Mednick, Martha Tamara Shuch, Sandra Schwartz Tangri, and Lois Wladis Hoffman, eds. **Women and Achievement: Social and Motivational Analyses.** New York: John Wiley & Sons, 1975.
The most detailed and well-documented treatment of women's educational and occupational achievement patterns published to date. Patterns of sex discrimination are dispassionately dealt with throughout the whole work.

Pleck, Joseph H., and Jack Sawyer, eds. **Men and Masculinity.** Englewood Cliffs, New Jersey: Prentice-Hall, 1974.
A thinly documented but highly suggestive analysis of the traditional male role.

/6/

A BIBLICAL CRITIQUE
OF TRADITIONAL SEX
ROLES

Scripture gives the framework by which people can understand their relationship to God, to others, and to themselves. But it is not simply a theological treatise or a code of ethics. Rather, the Bible is the record of God's acts in history—His patient dealings with rebellious people and His redemptive sacrifice for them. Scripture must be understood according to this purpose. Although it contains a message that is for all human beings in all times and places, the applications of that message are in terms of specific cultural and historical situations. The central redemptive message of Scripture is clear enough, but this does not mean that all of the Bible is equally understandable. Some of the problems in understanding Scripture are due to the very nature of the vehicle by which it was given—human language. Others are due to a lack of knowledge of the historical context in which it was written. We must always keep in mind the distinction between the divine character of Scripture and the human character of our understanding. The divine character of Scripture gives it an authority that we cannot claim for our understanding of it.

This perspective on Scripture points directly to some fundamental principles for interpreting it. First, because the Bible was written within specific cultural and historical contexts, it must be interpreted in terms of these contexts. We must ask many questions if we are to understand the context of a particular passage. Who wrote it? What was the human author's state of mind when he wrote it? Who were its recipients? What was its specific occasion? What was the political and social situation at the time? Is the message limited in time ("Bring my cloak") or timeless ("Love one another")? Is the author addressing some particular social injustice ("Masters, do not threaten your servants") or advocating a new social relationship ("There is no such thing as . . . slave and freeman . . . for you are all one person in Christ Jesus")? Is the author instructing his readers about a particular cultural custom of the day ("Wash one another's feet") or using that custom to illustrate an underlying transcultural principle of Christian behavior (the principle of serving one another)? The message of Scripture is incomplete and distorted unless it is interpreted in the context in which it was written.

A second principle of interpretation is that since Scripture was given to us in the vehicle of human language, it must be interpreted in a way that does justice to the nature of human language—its grammar, its syntax, its literary structures, its figures of speech, etc. Consequently, God's choice of human language to convey his revelation presents certain difficulties because of the very nature of human language. For instance, a word represents an area of meaning, not an exact point of meaning. Therefore even when we know the context in which a word is being used, we cannot always ascertain its precise meaning beyond doubt. Questions of morphology (the patterns of word formation in a particular language), syntax (the patterns of word order in sentences), and idiom must also be thoroughly considered in the interpretation of Scripture. It is possible to know the meanings of all the words in a particular sentence and still have difficulty understanding the meaning of the sentence.

The third principle of interpretation is that since Scripture contains a single, internally consistent body of truth, any passage of Scripture must be understood in terms of the context of all Scripture. The concept that Scripture is internally consistent does not negate the progressive character of God's revelation. It means however that Scripture does not contradict in one place what it teaches in another. At times, Scripture may appear to be inconsistent (e.g., there is no slave or freeman in Christ, and yet slaves are to obey their masters). Often we can understand this seeming inconsistency by distinguishing between the presentation of a principle of behavior and the implementation of a principle of behavior in a particular cultural situation. In any event, we may not interpret a given passage of Scripture in such a way as to bring it in conflict with other passages.

With this understanding of Scripture and its associated principles and problems of interpretation, we can now proceed to the biblical evidence bearing on traditional sex roles. First we must examine the relationship of females and males in Creation, in the Fall, and in redemption. What we find out can then serve as the foundation for a biblical critique of traditional female and male roles in American society.

Males and Females
in Creation

The first two chapters of Genesis are God's special revelation of His created order for the universe. The first passage bearing on the female-male relationship is Genesis 1:26-27 (all Scripture quotations in this chapter are from The New International Version unless otherwise noted):

> 26Then God said, "Let us make man in our image, in our likeness, and let them rule over the fish of the sea and the birds of the air, over the livestock, over all the earth, and over all the creatures that move along the ground."
> 27So God created man in his own image,
> in the image of God he created him;
> male and female he created them.

Here man is said to have been created in the image of God as male and female. Biblical scholars are far from agreement on the precise nature of the image of God spoken of in these verses. Some interpreters believe that the nature of the image of God is clarified by the cultural mandate that follows in verses 28 to 30.[1] God created man, both male and female, with the ability to manage and use the creation in a responsible fashion. Others define the concept "image of God" primarily by the expression immediately following it, "male and female."[2] Consequently, they believe that the image of God refers to the relational character of man; that is, that man was created as a "being-in-fellowship" whose mutuality and reciprocity reflects the relational character of the Godhead. Still others define "image" largely in terms of New Testament references like Colossians 3:10 and Ephesians 4:22-25.[3] These passages associate image with the knowledge of God, the righteousness and the holiness that are restored for all believers through Christ's redemptive act.

The image of God is mentioned only four times in the Old Testament, three times in the two verses just quoted and then again in Genesis 9:6—

> 6Whoever sheds the blood of man,

by man shall his blood be shed;
for in the image of God
has God made man.

In this verse the seriousness of killing another man is emphasized by the reference to man's being made in the image of God, a characteristic that clearly distinguishes him from the animals. The killing of a man, therefore, differs significantly from the killing of an animal.

Regardless of which interpretation of the "image of God" one chooses, two things are clear. First, man as male and female, in being created in God's image, was created as significantly different from the animals. Second, both females and males have been created in the image of God.

Several lines of argument have been advanced to suggest that though both males and females have been created in the image of God, they participate in that image in a different manner or to a different degree. One argument derives from the etymology of the two Hebrew words for male and female. However, that etymology is too obscure to support the idea of some difference between the sexes in the nature or extent of the image of God in them. Moreover, these two concepts are commonly used not only of man but of animals as well (Gen. 6:19; 7:3,9,16) and in these cases are used solely to distinguish a sexual difference. Consequently, it seems reasonable to say that these words refer only to the biological differences between women and men and do not imply any difference in their relative worth or in their participation in the image of God.[4]

Another argument rests on the fact that the male is mentioned first. Such a sequence, however, is customary regardless of whether the author is speaking of men or of animals. It should not be thought to indicate some type of priority or hierarchy.

A third argument is that both an equality and a hierarchy are present in the male-female relationship. In this view the image of God is divided into several components, some of which women share with men and some of which they do not. This was the approach taken by Calvin, who believed that women shared equally in the image of God spiritually but were not equal to men in their role in this present earthly order.[5] Such a division of the image of God appears to be completely unjustified on the basis of the Genesis narrative.

Scripture must also be understood as a corrective of the erroneous ideas present in pagan religions at the time it was written. In its account of the origin of maleness and femaleness, the Bible is in radical contrast to the polytheistic mythologies of that day. These mythologies view creation always in terms of procreation. Apparently the authors of these mythologies had difficulty conceiving of a creation in other than sexual terms. In contrast to this, the biblical view is that maleness and femaleness are a part of the original structure of Creation. Pagan mythologies (such as Enuma Elish) view creation as the product of forces that were sexual in character, while the biblical concept is that sexual differentiation was the result of the creative act of God.

To sum up, the conclusions that can be drawn from an examination of Genesis 1:26-27 are: (1) that sexual differentiation is a result of the original creative act of God, (2) that God distinguished man, male and female, from the rest of creation by creating him in the image of God, and (3) that males and females alike participate in that image so that there is no differentiation between the sexes in the essential quality of humanness. Furthermore, nothing in these verses supports the notion of an essential difference between women and men that would warrant any type of a relationship between them other than one of equality.

Genesis 2:18-24 has traditionally been interpreted in such a way as to speak to the relationship of males and females, and so we must examine this passage also.

[18]The Lord God said, "It is not good for the man to be alone. I will make a helper suitable for him."

[19]Now the Lord God had formed out of the ground all the beasts of the field and all the birds of the air. He brought them to the man to see what he would name them; and whatever the man called each living creature, that was its name. [20]So the man gave names to all the livestock, the birds of the air and all the beasts of the field.

But for Adam no suitable helper was found. [21]So the Lord God caused the man to fall into a deep sleep; and while he was sleeping, he took one of the man's ribs and closed up the place with flesh. [22]Then the Lord God made a woman from the rib he had taken out of the man, and he brought her to the man. [23]The man said,

"This is now bone of my bones
and flesh of my flesh;
she shall be called 'woman,'
for she was taken out of man."

[24]For this reason a man will leave his father and mother and be united to his wife, and they will become one flesh.

The first point usually made about this passage involves the use of the word *'ezer* in verse 18. This word is variously translated "help" (KJV), "helper" (RSV and NIV), and "partner" (NEB). The question is whether or not this concept in any sense denotes someone of lesser quality or ability. Today "help" or "helper" is generally used to refer to someone who assists a superior (a plumber's helper) or is under the direction or authority of someone else (hired help). It is easy, therefore, to read a dominant-subordinate character into the male-female relationship because of the use of *'ezer* in Genesis 2:18.

However, we must find out how the Bible itself uses this word. *'Ezer* occurs only twenty-one times in the Old Testament (Gen. 2:18,20; Exod. 18:4; Deut. 33:7,26,29; Ps. 20:2; 33:20; 70:5; 89:19; 115:9,10,11; 121:1,2; 124:8; 146:5; Isa. 30:5; Ezek. 12:14; Hos. 13:9; Dan. 11:34). The one to whom the word most often refers is God Himself. In its occurrences in the Pentateuch other than in Genesis

2 and in the majority of its occurrences elsewhere in the Old Testament, 'ezer refers to God. Since this word is used so frequently of God, contrasting the "help" of God to the "helplessness" of man, one can hardly suppose that it refers to an inferior or less able being in Genesis 2.

Another part of this narrative that bears on the female-male relationship is verses 21-24, which portray the chronological ordering of the origin of man and of woman. The question to be asked is whether or not this picture of the chronological sequence teaches, either implicitly or explicitly, a difference of ability, quality, or essence between the sexes. The text itself appears to help us answer the question. The man's response to the origin of woman is given in verse 23. Expressions similar to those in this verse are used elsewhere in the Old Testament (cf. Gen. 29:14; Judg. 9:2; 2 Sam. 5:1; 19:12,13) to indicate a blood relationship and, as Vos suggests, an "equality of being."[6]

The meaning of the last verse of this passage (v. 24) is apparent. Marriage is a relationship of mutuality between man and woman, of interdependence—an organic, "one flesh" relationship. "One flesh" denotes a unity, not a differentiation of being or quality.

Evangelical Christians have often interpreted aspects of Genesis 2 to suggest a superior-inferior relationship between men and women. For example, some have tried to support the superiority of the man in creation by pointing to verse 16, where God gives the man specific instructions about what he may and may not do in the garden. In the opinion of some, the fact that God did not wait and tell both the man and the woman at the same time implies a greater moral understanding or a more direct moral responsibility to God on the part of the male. It has been noted also that in verses 19 and 20 God places the responsibility of naming the animals on the man. This is thought by some to indicate, or at least imply, that the male was created with greater intellectual ability than the female.[7]

On the other hand, other aspects of the narrative could be used to suggest *female* superiority. For example, one could say that since the order of creation was from lower to higher, from the lesser to the greater, therefore the woman was the highest act of creation, since she was the last. Or one could note that the etymology of "man" refers to nonliving material, whereas the etymology of "Eve" refers to life (cf. Gen. 3:20), which is considered higher or more noble than nonlife. Or, by stretching one's exegetical imagination, one might suggest that femaleness actually predates maleness, for in Genesis 2:7 'adam (man) was formed from 'adamah (ground), same root but with feminine ending. Finally, one might point out that "the man" in verse 24 leaves his domicile to join his wife, implying a superiority of the female, since the normal practice in marriage customs around the world is that the less important person joins the more important one.

All these attempts to find a superiority-inferiority relationship of man and woman in Genesis 2 appear to require of the narrative a meaning that is either completely foreign to it or at the very most peripheral to its essential meaning. The attempts reflect more the biases of the interpreters than the message of Scripture.

In summary, the creation narrative in Genesis 1 and 2 contains three dominant themes about female and male relationships. First is the equality of man and woman in creation. They participate equally in the image of God, that is, they share equally an essential humanness and they share equally a distinctiveness from the animals. Second, there is the theme of a differentiation in the creation of mankind—for he was created "male and female." This differentiation is not of essence, or being, but rather of biology. The last theme of the creation narrative is that of unity—for man and woman constitute "one flesh." In God's sight the two have an essential oneness, a oneness of such a character that Christ gives stern warning regarding its dissolution (Matt. 19:6; Mark 10:9).

Before we examine the Fall as recorded in Genesis 3, it may be useful to attempt to picture the nature of marriage and society that would have resulted from the creation order of Genesis 1 and 2 had there been no sin. Although this is obviously speculative, it may bring into focus more clearly the effects of the curse on man and woman and the type of male-female relationships that subsequently developed.

Most likely there would have been a differentiation of female and male tasks in society. This, though not explicitly stated in the narrative, can be inferred as the expected consequence of the sexual differences that God created. By virtue of their created sexual differences, men and women would of course have played different reproductive roles, and the reproductive differences probably would have led to different social roles. Women's social participation would have been somewhat limited because of pregnancy; being pregnant limits the kind and amount of physical activity a woman can do. Women's activities would also have been limited by the necessity of nursing small children; nursing limits the mother's mobility, keeping her in the vicinity of the home. Consequently, women probably would have taken on the tasks easily combined with the care of small children and household maintenance, whereas men would likely have been responsible for the tasks demanding greater physical strength and geographical mobility such as hunting. All other social activities could easily have been shared.

The impact of the created reproductive differences on social activities probably would have extended to decision making. Because of his greater geographical mobility, the male would have been involved in a wider range of activities than the female. That range of activities would have included more contacts with people outside his immediate group. Therefore decisions involving the relation of his immediate social unit (his family) to other social units (whether other families or larger groups) would probably have fallen to him. Decisions having to do with the day-to-day care of children and maintenance of the household would probably have been made by the female. Many other decisions would have been made mutually.

This division of social tasks and associated areas of decision making that might—we speculate—have developed had there not been a Fall would not have been due to different "qualities" inherent in males and females. Genesis 1 and 2 do not indicate such differences. It is also important to recognize that this division of labor would have been present within an egalitarian family structure. There is no necessary link between a division of labor and a hierarchical structure in a social unit. The division of labor speculated on here would simply have been the result of the created reproductive differences; it would not have been inconsistent with the intended "one flesh" relationship between the husband and the wife.

Females and Males in the Fall

The created order for the relationship of males and females was radically altered by the ensuing events of human history. Adam and Eve originally lived harmoniously with their Creator, with the creation, and with each other. They knew what was expected of them. But they disobeyed, and their disobedience ruptured their relationship to God. Man sought to hide from God, thus picturing for us the spiritual separation that was the inevitable product of disobedience. God's displeasure was manifest in the curse he placed on the serpent, the woman, and the man. The general theme of Genesis 3 is that when man loses his proper relationship to God, he also loses his proper relationships in all aspects of his existence—to nature, to normal responsibilities, and to other persons.

Genesis 3 is not intended to give us an exhaustive picture of all the areas of life that are affected by the Fall; the Fall has ramifications for every aspect of life. However, it does picture certain central areas, and one of these is the relationship of women and men. The most explicit part of the curse regarding this relationship is in Genesis 3:16.

> [16]To the woman he said,
>   "I will greatly increase your pains in childbearing;
>   with pain will you give birth to children.
> Your desire will be for your husband,
>   and he will rule over you."

This verse contains two couplets. In the first couplet, the woman is told by God that because she has lost her proper relationship to God, normal human experiences such as childbirth will henceforth involve a degree of pain that was not originally intended. This idea is brought out clearly in the expression "I will greatly increase your pains."

The second couplet (lines 3 and 4) speaks explicitly about the impact of the Fall on the male-female relationship (in the context of the family). The woman is told that her "desire" will be for her husband. The Hebrew expression here is a rare one that occurs only two other times in the Old Testament—in the Song of Solomon 7:11, where it seems to have a sexual connotation, and in Genesis 4:7, where it does not (Cain is warned by God that sin "desires" to have him). Hence interpretations vary. Those believing that the expression has a sexual connotation tend to interpret line 3 in terms of lines 1 and 2[8]; that is, the woman will face the agonizing dilemma of being eager for sexual relations with her husband while at the same time she knows that the result of her gratification, bearing children, will be a painful experience.

Other interpretations take line 3 as related in meaning more closely to line 4 than to line 2. One such interpretation is suggested by Vos, who says that the woman, "because she has less physical strength, will desire the man for protection after she is banned from the garden and placed in a hostile world in which brutality and force are the order of the day." [9] This desire, he adds, has as a result the fact that man will rule over her.

Another possible interpretation refers the desire, not to physical protection, but to eagerness to please the man—that is, to seek to continue the harmonious relationship of husband and wife that they had experienced before they sinned. This interpretation implies that, even when she does all she can to maintain the original relationship, her husband is going to extend the areas of his decision making beyond those associated with his original responsibilities. This extension will gradually but persistently impinge on the decision-making areas associated with her original tasks until he has a sphere of authority and jurisdiction that was not his by creation. In this interpretation, line 3 implies that, regardless of the effort she makes, and regardless of her willingness and motivation, she will find herself with a shrinking area of decision making. The ultimate result will be that the man will "rule over her." [10] If the man had this kind of authority by creation, then these words would be superfluous. They must be understood to indicate some significant change in the relationship as the result of sin. In other words, an egalitarian husband-wife relationship will be replaced by a hierarchical one in which the husband is dominant and takes a prominent role.

Certain details of this narrative suggest to some interpreters that a hierarchical relationship between man and woman existed prior to the Fall and that because of the curse it changed from a kindly hierarchy into a despotic rule. [11] One of these details is that the serpent tempted the woman rather than the man. Therefore, the argument goes, she must have taken God's commands less seriously than her husband did, or she was more vulnerable than he, or possibly she realized that her character was weaker than his and that by eating the fruit of the tree of the knowledge of good and evil she would raise herself to equality with him. Another suggestion is that when God addressed them (3:9) he spoke to the man first, as if he was in charge, and then to the woman.

These suggestions, though interesting, are far from persuasive. The basic picture is not clear in detail, but it does appear to have some clarity in general outline. According to this outline, when man disobeyed, thus separating himself from God, this loss of a proper relationship with God resulted in a loss of man's original harmonious relationship to all aspects of his experience. A part of this is the male-female relationship. The curse is not intended to be a cataloging of all the places where the effects of sin would be felt; rather, it speaks of certain major or representative areas of activity.

From this point in history women began to experience a subordination that was not a part of the creation order. This subordination was at times vicious and at times benign, but only rarely absent. Man, from his very biological nature and from the roles that ordinarily fall to him, almost always occupies a position that enables him to encroach upon those areas that the woman occupies by virtue of her biological makeup and the roles that normally fall to her. Thus the egalitarian structure ordained by creation was changed into a hierarchical structure because of man's sin.

Two further questions about this passage need to be considered. The first is this: Is God, by his pronouncement of the curse, establishing a new normative pattern for the relationship of husband and wife? Or is God merely informing them of the consequences that will result from their fall? If one accepts the first alternative— that God is establishing a new normative pattern—then the pattern of husband-wife relations ordained by Creation is of no great importance to us, except from the standpoint of historical interest. A new pattern has been established, and the old has been phased out. The new type of relationship would stand before us as the new normative pattern, the ideal for which one should strive. If one accepts the second alternative—that God is informing them of the consequences that will result from their sin—then one views this new pattern as a distortion and a corruption of the original. It is a pattern that results from man's sinful nature rather than from the will of God. Then when one is renewed in Christ, as Paul speaks of in Ephesians 4:23, this pattern would begin changing back to the form it had in Creation. This transformation obviously is neither automatic nor instantaneous, being totally realized only in God's eternal kingdom. However, it would remain as the ideal to be pursued as we live our new life in Christ. In short, the second alternative views the dominance-subordination pattern that we see throughout the Old Testament as a perversion of the pattern of Creation, the natural consequence of alienation from God.

The second question is this: Is this new male-dominant/female-subordinate pattern to be realized only in the husband-wife relationship, or will it also be realized in the broader male-female relationship within society? It would appear that this question cannot be answered from the text, since the only male-female relationship spoken of there is that of marriage. One can conceive of a society with a sexual hierarchy in the family and not in society, though that would be unlikely. The safer interpretation would apply this verse only to the male-female relationship within the family, while at the same time realizing that the larger social system would almost inevitably exhibit a similar hierarchical pattern.

Males and Females
in Redemption

Although man by his own free will had alienated himself from God, his Creator did not desert him. God provided for man the means by which that broken relationship could be healed and the alienation replaced by fellowship. The redemptive act of Christ was more than sufficient to counteract the results of Adam's sin in the world. This is clearly set forth in both Romans 5 and 1 Corinthians 15. Romans 5:15-19 reads:

> But the gift is not like the trespass. For if the many died by the trespass of the one man, how much more did God's grace and the gift that came by the grace of the one man, Jesus Christ, overflow to the many! Again, the gift of God is not like the result of the one man's sin: The judgment followed one sin and brought condemnation, but the gift followed many trespasses and brought justification. For if, by the trespass of the one man, death reigned through that one man, how much more will those who receive God's abundant provision of grace and of the gift of righteousness reign in life through the one man, Jesus Christ.
>
> Consequently, just as the result of one trespass was condemnation for all men, so also the result of one act of righteousness was justification that brings life for all men. For just as through the disobedience of the one man the many were made sinners, so also through the obedience of the one man the many will be made righteous.

The results of Christ's work have a direct bearing on the consequences of Adam's sin. The broken relationship that resulted from Adam's sin is now replaced by a life of fellowship in Christ. This means not only that we are offered forgiveness for Adam's sin but also that Christ's redemptive work has a healing effect on the ramifications of the Fall in all areas of our lives. Since one of the consequences of Adam's sin was the development of a dominant-submissive relationship that was foreign to the character of male-female relationships in Creation, the redemptive work of Christ will affect the nature of those relationships. Christ's work will have a restorative or corrective influence in this area. This obviously does not mean that male and female roles will disappear or that the reproductive differences between the sexes will come to have less effect on those roles. What it means is that the spheres of activities and responsibilities and the harmonious relationship that woman and man originally had in Creation will be more fully realized.

The work of Christ does not in any simple or automatic fashion eliminate the effects of sin in our lives or in the world. Still, those effects should diminish as people grow in the Christian faith and as the process of sanctification affects more and more areas of their lives.

The passage most frequently quoted as biblical evidence of the restorative impact of Christ's redemptive work on the male-female relationship is Galatians 3:26-28—

> [26]You are all sons of God through faith in Christ Jesus, [27]for all of you who were united with Christ in baptism have been clothed with Christ. [28]There is neither Jew nor Greek, slave nor free, male nor female, for you are all one in Christ Jesus.

These verses are a part of a section in which Paul is contrasting for the Galatians their new condition in Christ with their old condition before Christ. The central message appears to be that all those distinctions between people that previously were sources of alienation and separation have been superseded by their union in Christ. These distinctions were matters of nationality (Jew or Greek), social status (slave or free man), and sexuality (male or female). This verse doesn't mean that such differences will cease to exist among Christians; what it means is that they will not separate people out for different treatment or recognition in Christ. In other words, believers' oneness in Christ supersedes their human differences. Yet the differences will continue to exist, and consequently the different roles will continue to exist.

Some might argue that Galatians 3:28 implies that there should be a total elimination of the difference in the roles that males and females fill, with their associated tasks and responsibilities. But total elimination is not required by this text, nor can it be carried out on the practical level, because of the created differences between males and females. Having different roles does not inevitably imply or produce a dominance-submission relationship. Verse 29, "If you belong to Christ, then you are Abraham's seed, and so heirs according to the promise," specifically associates the lack of distinctions noted in verse 28 with the idea that believers are equally "heirs by promise."

In summary, verse 28 cannot be used to support the case that there should be no role differentiation of any kind between the sexes either within the family or outside it. Its primary message is that all people, regardless of nationality, social status, and sex, may be equally the children of God by virtue of their union with Christ and thus equally "heirs by promise."

Now that we have examined the general character of the female-male relationship in the redemptive order, we can move to those passages in the New Testament that speak directly about marriage. First, Ephesians 5:21-33.

21Submit to one another out of reverence for Christ.

22Wives, submit to your husbands as to the Lord. 23For the husband is the head of the wife as Christ is the head of the church, his body, of which he is the Savior. 24Now as the church submits to Christ, so also wives should submit to their husbands in everything.

25Husbands, love your wives, just as Christ loved the church and gave himself up for her 26to make her holy, cleansing her by the washing with water through the word, 27and to present her to himself as a radiant church, without stain or wrinkle or any other blemish, but holy and blameless. 28In this same way, husbands ought to love their wives as their own bodies. He who loves his wife loves himself. 29After all, no one ever hated his own body, but he feeds and cares for it, just as Christ does the church— 30for we are members of his body. 31"For this reason a man will leave his father and mother and will be united to his wife, and the two will become one flesh." 32This is a profound mystery—but I am talking about Christ and the church. [33]However, each one of you also must love his wife as he loves himself, and the wife must respect her husband.

The context of this passage is that Paul is instructing the Ephesians about the practical applications of their new life in Christ. The first part of chapter 5 is a set of instructions applicable to all new believers, whatever their sex and social position. Then follows a section—5:21 to 6:9—in which Paul talks specifically about relationships in the home, first between husband and wife, then between parents and children, and finally between slaves and masters.

Traditionally, two approaches have been taken to the verses in Ephesians 5 about husbands and wives. The first approach, which is by far the most common, interprets these verses as speaking primarily of the relationship of men as husbands to women as wives. This approach emphasizes such expressions as "the husband is the head of the wife" and "a wife should submit unto her husband in everything." Men and women are viewed as fundamentally different with respect to decision-making authority. Supporters of this view also point out that the relationship of the wife and the husband is parallel to the relationship of the church and Christ. Christ is the head of the church; the husband is the head of the wife. The church's responsibility is to serve its Lord; the wife's responsibility is to serve her husband. The church owes its very existence to Christ; the woman's very existence is derived from the man. As a result, man and woman are not equal in origin, in responsibility, or in authority. The picture derived with this approach is one of a clear hierarchy between husband and wife.

A second way of interpreting this passage is to emphasize the headship of Christ as ultimately a "headship" of service. Christ as head of the church gave Himself up for it, to consecrate it, cleansing it by water and the word, so that He might present the church to Himself all glorious, with no stain or wrinkle or anything of the sort, but holy and without blemish (Eph. 5:25-27). This approach emphasizes that the basic role of Christ was not one of being ministered unto but of ministering to others (cf. Matt. 20:28). This interpretation certainly softens the character of the hierarchical relationship, but it does not change the essential structure of it, for the husband is still the "head" and the responsibility of the wife is still to "submit."

There is, however, a third interpretation that in many ways is more consistent with the broader context of this passage. In the first three chapters of the book, Paul speaks of God's plan of salvation through the redemptive work of Christ and the indwelling work of the Holy Spirit, by which the Jews and the pagans are reconciled both to God and to one another. Therefore the church includes radically different types of people—Jews and Gentiles, males and females, young and old, members of different ethnic groups, people of different social classes. A fundamental problem for this new church was how to integrate such diverse people into a united fellowship, one not divided by the differences that separated its members in society. So Paul begins chapter 4 with a call to unity, saying, in verses 3-6:

> [3]Make every effort to keep the unity of the Spirit through the bond of peace. [4]There is one body and one Spirit—just as you were called to one hope when you were called— [5]one Lord, one faith, one baptism; [6]one God and Father of all, who is over all and through all and in all.

Paul continues telling the believers that they are not to achieve this unity by denying or disregarding individual differences or gifts. He says in verses 7 and 11-13:

> [7]But to each one of us grace has been given as Christ apportioned it. . . . [11]It was he who gave some to be apostles, some to be prophets, some to be evangelists, and some to be pastors and

teachers, [12]to prepare God's people for works of service, so that the body of Christ may be built up [13]until we all reach unity in the faith and in the knowledge of the Son of God and become mature, attaining the full measure of perfection found in Christ.

And if each person performs her or his particular God-given activities, the larger group will function as a united whole—a body with Christ as the head in which each separate part makes its contribution:

[15]Instead, speaking the truth in love, we will in all things grow up into him who is the Head, that is, Christ. [16]From him the whole body, joined and held together by every supporting ligament, grows and builds itself up in love, as each part does its work.

Such unity is the ideal and thus the goal for which Christians should strive, but the realization of the ideal meets many obstacles. How can such unity be achieved out of such diverse parts?

Paul provides an answer to this question by using the metaphor of the human body. Here we realize the differences are enormous. Some parts are visible (ears), others not (pancreas); some are obviously important (heart), others not so (twelfth rib); some have a controlling function (pituitary gland), others a controlled function (salivary glands); some are absolutely necessary for life (lungs), while others are not (third molars). How can parts that differ so in visibility, function, and indispensability be united into a functional unity? The answer lies in the recognition that each makes its unique contribution to the whole. Visible parts do not reduce the need for the unseen parts. The more important organs do not negate the contribution of the apparently less important ones.

Precisely the same situation exists in the body of Christ. Some persons are very visible; others remain unseen. Some are obviously important, others less obviously so. Some receive recognition, while others live in obscurity. This is not because of a difference in intrinsic worth or ultimate importance but because of the nature of role differentiation in social groups.

But this role differentiation creates certain practical problems. The persons who have roles that are highly visible, obviously important, and well recognized by society tend to assume a position of dominance and authority that is not rightfully theirs. And persons whose roles have low visibility and recognition feel, on the one hand, a sense of worthlessness and, on the other, jealousy and antagonism toward those in more prominent roles.

The solution to this problem is the same whether the body is the human body or the "body of Christ": each part must be recognized, regardless of visibility and outward importance, as making a unique contribution to the whole. Each part must perform its particular responsibilities in a selfless manner—not assuming an importance beyond that which is legitimate, not belittling the contributions of others, not exerting an undue authority, and not resisting the legitimate authority of others. It is true, both within the body of Christ and outside it, that a position of authority carries with it the potential for abuse of that authority. It is also true that the position of being under the authority of others carries with it the potential danger of resisting that authority even though it is legitimate.

To summarize, there is an inherent difficulty in the very nature of role differentiation and the differential distribution of authority. That difficulty can be resolved only when those who have roles of authority exercise that authority with utmost concern for the subordinates, and when those who do not have roles of authority willingly submit to those who do. Only then can the organization function with a sense of unity, cooperation, and harmony.

This is the particular problem with which Paul is concerned in Ephesians 5 and 6. He deals with it by examining three pairs of complementary roles, in each of which a differential in authority was ascribed in that culture. For all three cases the instructions are essentially the same.

The first example is that of husbands and wives. Paul was writing to couples living in a society in which there was a sharp difference in social position between the husband and the wife. The husband was dominant, the wife subordinate. To those with the dominant role Paul says: "Love your wives, just as Christ loved the church" (v. 25) because "no one ever hated his own body, but he feeds and cares for it" (v. 29). In other words, these men are to use the role of husband, not as a position of power in which they extend the boundaries of their existing authority, but rather as a position of service. Their authority is to be exercised ultimately for the welfare of the family and not for their own gratification. The wives, in their subordinate role in this culture, are not to perform their tasks feeling antagonistic or hostile toward their husbands because they have been assigned a "less important" role. They are not to resist authority or to be uncooperative as a way of getting even with legitimate authority. In Paul's words, wives are to submit to and respect their husbands.

The second example is that of children and parents. Here again the two roles have a difference in authority ascribed to them. Paul tells those in the subordinate role (children) to be obedient; those in the dominant role he tells not to exercise their authority in such a way as to alienate the subordinate ones.

The third example is slaves and masters, and again the instructions are basically the same. Those in the subordinate social role are to "obey (their) earthly masters with respect and fear, and with sincerity of heart just as (they) would obey Christ" (Eph. 6:5). Those in the dominant social role are to exercise the authority associated with their role in the spirit of Christ, not by the use of threats.

Therefore, a possible understanding of this passage is that Paul is not specifying some universal, timeless norms regarding the relationship of husbands and wives, of children and parents, and of slaves and masters. Instead, Paul may be warning against certain obstacles to unity, obstacles inherent in the very nature of social systems in which various roles carry significantly different amounts of authority. In other words, he is not attempting to articulate the proper place of men and women in society but rather is giving a warning about those points where the unity of the group tends to break down. This interpretation seems particularly compelling given the fact that in the larger context of these statements Paul is addressing the problems of obtaining unity out of diversity in the body of Christ.

There are two additional reasons for accepting this interpretation of the Ephesians passage rather than the other two presented earlier. First, Paul's final statement in this passage (Eph. 6:9) indicates that God is not impressed by one person more than another: "You know that he who is both their Master and yours is in heaven, and there is no favoritism with him" (Eph. 6:9). Paul is referring specifically to masters and slaves here, but given the Galatians 3 passage, the statement would be equally applicable to parents and children and to husbands and wives. Paul is reminding Christians that one person is not more important than another, nor does one person's role carry greater dignity in God's sight than another's, nor does any human characteristic, whether social status, age, or sex, place one on a higher pedestal before God. Rather, all positions and the people occupying them have equal dignity in the eyes of God.

The second reason for accepting this interpretation stems from Paul's initial statement in the passage: "Submit to one another out of reverence for Christ" (Eph.

5:21). At first glance this appears to be contradicted immediately as Paul begins to speak of dominant and subordinate roles. Yet this principle of mutual subjection (found also in Philippians 2:3 and in 1 Peter 5:5) appears to be the more basic idea, in view of its priority in the passage. Submitting here means being selfless, that is, seeking to serve others rather than oneself regardless of one's role or standing in the social system. In its context, which is an exhortation to unity, this verse seems to mean that each person is to submit himself or herself in a serving way by faithfully fulfilling his or her particular role in the society, so that the unity that should characterize the body of Jesus Christ can be achieved.

Two other passages in the New Testament speak specifically about the relationship of women and men in marriage. The first, Colossians 3:18-19, closely parallels the Ephesians passage but is much briefer:

> [18]Wives, submit to your husbands, as is fitting in the Lord. [19]Husbands, love your wives and do not be harsh with them.

Again Paul is speaking about their new life in Christ and giving general instructions regarding Christian behavior. He speaks of the same three sets of complementary roles—husband-wife, parent-child, and master-slave—and gives the same instructions. These instructions again must be seen within the larger context, which is the matter of achieving unity in the body of Christ. In the same chapter we read:

> [11]Here there is no Greek or Jew, circumcised or uncircumcised, barbarian, Scythian, slave or free, but Christ is all, and is in all.... [14]And over all these virtues put on love, which binds them all together in perfect unity. [15]Let the peace of Christ rule in your hearts, since, as members of one body, you were called to peace. And be thankful.

To achieve this unity, those in dominant roles are instructed to exercise those roles with love, gentleness, fairness, and justice, while those in subordinate roles are instructed to be submissive, respectful, and obedient.

The final passage that speaks explicitly of the husband-wife relationship is 1 Peter 3:1-7.

> [1]Wives, in the same way be submissive to your husbands so that, if any of them do not believe the word, they may be won over without talk by the behavior of their wives, [2]when they see the purity and reverence of your lives. [3]Your beauty should not come from outward adornment, such as braided hair and the wearing of gold jewelry and fine clothes. [4]Instead, it should be that of your inner self, the unfading beauty of a gentle and quiet spirit, which is of great worth in God's sight. [5]For this is the way the holy women of the past who put their hope in God used to make themselves beautiful. They were submissive to their own husbands, [6]like Sarah, who obeyed Abraham and called him her master. You are her daughters if you do what is right and do not give way to fear.
>
> [7]Husbands, in the same way be considerate as you live with your wives, and treat them with respect as the weaker partner and as heirs with you of the gracious gift of life, so that nothing will hinder your prayers.

In this letter Peter is instructing new believers. They are to be living stones in a spiritual house of which Christ himself is the cornerstone (2:4-10). Together they form a united structure, "a chosen race, a royal priesthood, a dedicated nation, and a people claimed by God for his own" (2:9). In that structure, the characteristics that separate people in society and alienate them from one another are not important. However, in the society in which they live, these distinctions continue to exist because they are inevitable in social systems. In order to attempt to realize the unity that Christians have in Christ, each one must willingly accept his particular social roles and responsibilities. In 2:13-17 Peter speaks of these Christians' responsibilities to the civil authorities and in 2:18-25 of the mutual responsibilities of slaves and masters. Then in 3:1-7 he comments on the relationship of husband and wife. Again, wives are instructed to be obedient and husbands to be loving and considerate.

So Peter, like Paul, is addressing the threats to unity that are inherent in any dominant-subordinate relationship, whether political, economic, or familial. Those threats are the misuse of authority by the dominant and insubordination by the subordinates. In this passage Peter adds one motivation for wives to follow his instructions that Paul did not mention: the manner in which a wife fulfills her role may lead to the conversion of an unbelieving spouse.

The three New Testament passages dealing with the male-female relationship in marriage, then, are very similar. The context is the same: a discussion of how to achieve unity in the body of Christ. The problem is the same: how to unite Christians with different gifts, different personal and social characteristics, and different amounts of authority based on their culturally assigned social roles. Finally, the prescribed solution to the problem is the same: the believers are to fulfill the expectations of their culturally assigned roles in as selfless or submissive a manner as possible. They are not to abuse their authority but are to show love. They are not to be insubordinate to legitimate authority but are to submit to it. They are to recognize that all Christians, regardless of their roles in society, are of equal value in God's sight and should be treated so in the body of Christ.

The basic message of these three passages of Scripture for us today, therefore, is not that there is a God-ordained, timeless hierarchy of authority between husbands and wives, parents and children, and slaves and masters. The message, rather, is that a certain selfless service orientation toward others, coupled with an affirmation of the ultimate equal worth of all persons, is required of Christians in order to achieve unity in the body of Christ.

This interpretation maintains that these three passages cannot be used to support the notion of a God-ordained division of authority between husbands and wifes, parents and children, and masters and slaves. It does not maintain, however, that there is no such normative division of authority in these three pairs of relationships. Therefore it is not inconsistent to hold to a timeless, God-ordained division of authority in the case of parent and child but not in the case of master and slave. The point is that an argument for such a division of authority in any of the three relationships must be established on the basis of other biblical passages, not these.

Many evangelical Christians might find themselves comfortable with this interpretation except for one thing—Paul's use of the term *head*[12] in conjunction with the statement that wives are to be subject to their husbands:

> [22]Wives, submit to your husbands as to the Lord. [23]For the husband is the head of the wife as Christ is the head of the church, his body, of which he is the Savior. [24]Now as the church submits to Christ, so also wives should submit to their husbands in everything (Eph. 5:22-23).

This is the only time in the New Testament that the concept of "husband as head" is attached to the wife's subjection. The only other time *head* is used in connection with the female-male relationship is in 1 Corinthians 11:3. Here the husband is spoken of as "head," but no specific mention is made of the wife's subjection:

> Now I want you to realize that the head of every man is Christ, and the head of the woman is man, and the head of Christ is God.

Many Christians have understood *head* in these passages to mean that the husband is to be in authority over the wife, and then have incorporated this conception of *head* into their basic beliefs about God's intentions for the male-female relationship. Before reaching a conclusion on these two passages, we need to examine the uses of *head* elsewhere in Scripture.

The word *head (kephale)* is used seventy-five times in the New Testament and in highly diverse ways. The first and most obvious meaning of the word is literal: the physical head of a person or animal (e.g., Matt. 14:8; 27:37; Mark 15:19; John 19:30). Sometimes *head* stands for the entire person (e.g., Matthew 27:25, "your blood be upon your heads," and Romans 12:20, "heap coals of fire on his head").

In addition to its literal use, *head* is often used in Scripture in a symbolic or metaphorical sense. Its variations in meaning are particularly evident in these uses. One such meaning is priority—a priority that may be due to a logical sequence (God the Father as head of the Son), a geographical sequence (head of a river), or other sorts of sequences. Used this way, the word could be translated origin, source, or even reason for being. Such a usage appears in Colossians 1:18:

> And he is the head of the body, the church; he is the beginning and the firstborn from among the dead, so that in everything he might have the supremacy.

Another figurative use of *head* implies a hierarchical arrangement, that is, a relationship of higher-lower, inferior-superior. This is exemplified in the relationship of Christ to Creation in Ephesians 1 and Colossians 1. Often associated with this use is the idea of sovereignty, jurisdiction, or dominion:

> . . .[19]and his incomparably great power for us who believe. That power is like the working of his mighty strength, [20]which he exerted in Christ when he raised him from the dead and seated him at his right hand in the heavenly realms, [21]far above all rule and authority, power and dominion, and every title that can be given, not only in the present age but also in the one to come. [22]And God placed all things under his feet and appointed him to be head over everything for the church, [23]which is his body, the fullness of him who fills everything in every way (Eph. 1:19-23).

Another use of head emphasizes the idea of complementarity:

> [14]Now the body is not made up of one part but of many. [15]If the

foot should say, "Because I am not a hand, I do not belong to the body," it would not for that reason cease to be part of the body. [16]And if the ear should say, "Because I am not an eye, I do not belong to the body," it would not for that reason cease to be part of the body (1 Cor. 12:14-16).

Here the parts of the head are not pictured as the higher or sovereign organs, or even the most important organs. They are portrayed merely as organs that share with all the other organs a mutual necessity, a complementarity. Closely associated with this idea, but slightly different, is the idea of unity or completeness. A bodiless head is as incomplete as a headless body. Christ without the church is as anomalous as the church without Christ. But Christ and the church together constitute a union—a meaningful, functional unity.

There are also places in Scripture where the functional unity of the head and body is directly attributed to the head. Such a place is Ephesians 4:15-16:

[15]Instead, speaking the truth in love, we will in all things grow up into him who is the Head, that is, Christ. [16]From him the whole body, joined and held together by every supporting ligament, grows and builds itself up in love, as each part does its work.

In this passage the head is spoken of not simply as another organ and a contributor to the unity of the body but as the source of that unity.

Yet another meaning associated with *head* is the idea of service. This is present in Ephesians 5:23-30, where Christ is spoken of as the head of the church:

[23]Christ is the head of the church, his body. . . . [25]Christ loved the church and gave himself up for her [26]to make her holy, cleansing her by the washing with water through the word. . . . [29]no one ever hated his own body, but he feeds and cares for it, just as Christ does the church—[30]for we are members of his body.

In these verses the head saves, cleanses, and cares for the body. The relationship between the head and the body is pictured as one of service from the head to the body, not the reverse.

Another meaning associated with *head* is goal or end development. This is evident in Ephesians 4:13-15:

> [13]until we all reach unity in the faith and in the knowledge of the Son of God and become mature, attaining the full measure of perfection found in Christ.
>
> [14]Then we will no longer be infants, tossed back and forth by the waves, and blown here and there by every wind of teaching and by the cunning and craftiness of men in their deceitful scheming. [15]Instead, speaking the truth in love, we will in all things grow up into him who is the Head, that is, Christ.

Here the head is presented as the goal of the body. The orientation of the body is to grow into Christ, the Head.

Yet even attending to all the ways in which *head* is used and the implications of these uses does not do complete justice to the idea as used in the New Testament. People in New Testament times did not view the head as necessarily the most important part of the body. They did not think of the head as the thinking or decision-making organ; that was the function of the heart. Nor was the head primarily pictured as the controlling organ with a brain instructing muscles to engage in various activities via nerve connections. The distinctiveness of the head was that it was the means by which the body primarily (not totally, but primarily) communicated with the world outside itself. Most contact with the outside world was through the head—both in giving messages (speech, facial gestures) and in receiving them (sight, smell, hearing). Consequently, the head served as the primary representative of the body in its relations with the outside world. In Matthew 6:17, Acts 18:18, and Revelation 18:19, the head is associated with the rituals of fasting and penitence. Moreover, the head bears the tokens of honor and dignity (e.g., Rev. 4:4; 19:12) and also those of shame (Rev. 13:1). In the act of ordination the hands are placed on the head.[13]

So it is necessary to keep in mind that the word *head* is used with varying meanings—an anatomical meaning, a sociological meaning, and a theological meaning. And while there are certain parallels between its use in one sense and its use in another sense, and these parallels may be instructive, we must not push them too far. It is obviously inappropriate to apply the idea of the head as the "goal" of the body when the word *head* is being used in an anatomical or sociological sense. And it is equally inappropriate to define *head* in a theological sense when one is referring to the anatomical head. Interpreting this concept in a particular passage requires a careful examination of the context.

However, to say that *head* has many meanings does not answer the question about these passages in which the husband is described as the head of the wife. Because of the many connotations of *head,* the interpretation it is given in the context of the man-woman relationship is largely a matter of the interpreter's preferences as well as his basic sociological orientation. To make the relationship hierarchical, the interpreter emphasizes the places where the concept carries the connotations of authority and sovereignty. To emphasize the equality of women and men, he uses the passages that speak about mutuality and complementarity. To establish that men and women are ordained for different roles in society, he cites the texts that associate *head* with service and representation. No amount of exegesis is going to resolve the issue in the same way for all people.

Despite this problem, let us return to the two passages that speak of the man as the head of the woman and attempt to determine the most likely area of meaning for *head* in each case. In the 1 Corinthians passage, Paul is instructing these Christians in the matter of proper conduct at public worship services. In this context he states:

> Now I want you to realize that the head of every man is Christ,

and the head of the woman is man, and the head of Christ is God (1 Cor. 11:3).

Here the word describes three relationships—Christ-man, husband-wife, and God-Christ. None of the meanings of *head* fits equally well for all three sets of relationships. Some of its meanings fit one set but not the others. Moreover, Paul has not arranged the three relationships in ascending or descending order. The single meaning that seems to be most generally applicable is priority (or origin, or source): in the first set a priority of rule, in the second set a priority of time, in the third set a priority of logical relationship. The view that priority of time is the primary meaning of *head* in the context of the husband-wife relationship (i.e., that man predates woman) seems to be supported by verse 8 of this chapter: "For man did not come from woman, but woman from man" (1 Cor. 11:8).

It is important to note that priority of time cannot be associated here with hierarchy because this verse is followed by verses 11 and 12, which speak of the woman and man's interdependence and complementarity:

> [11]In the Lord, however, woman is not independent of man, nor is man independent of woman. [12]For as woman came from man, so also man is born of woman. But everything comes from God.

The Ephesians 5 passage is found within that larger context in which Paul is issuing a call to unity. The instructions regarding husbands and wives, parents and children, and masters and slaves are an aspect of this call. The husband is the head of the wife as Christ is the head of the church. In this context, Christ's being the head of the church means that He saves the church (v. 23), sacrifices Himself for it (v. 25), and cleanses it (v. 25). Here headship primarily refers to service. Therefore, in this passage, as in 1 Corinthians 11:3, headship is not primarily associated with authority, decision making, sovereignty, or rule.

But to establish that headship in the male-female relationship is more closely linked with the ideas of service and origin does not fully resolve the issue. What sort of service is included in the role of headship? Does the male exercise this role simply because woman was derived from man? In fact, we still have three unanswered questions: (1) What, precisely, is the nature of headship in the context of the male-female relationship? (2) Why is headship attributed to the male? (3) In what sphere(s) of activity is male headship a legitimate functional principle—the family, the society, the church?

The answer to the first question may primarily be derived from the earlier discussion of the male-female relationship in Creation. In nonmodern societies—which were, of course, the only ones Paul knew—the male characteristically has more contacts with social units outside the immediate family. In his interaction with these groups he acts on behalf of his family. In other words, he becomes their representative—their mouth, their eyes, their ears. His role as head (representative) of the family to the broader society is analogous to that which an anatomical head plays in relation to the body. The decisions he makes that affect his family he makes by virtue of this representative role, not strictly by virtue of his sex. At times, because of the absence or incapacity of a husband, a wife must function as head and make the decisions associated with that role. It is doubtful, then, that Paul, on a practical level, saw an *inevitable* association between being the husband and being the family head, but certainly he saw this as the more logical association.

Unfortunately, this role of headship (whether exercised by the husband or by the wife) always has the potential of becoming a perverted form of headship in which the functioning head exercises that role in a selfish rather than selfless manner. Paul recognized this, and so he pointedly instructs husbands that they are to love their wives just as Christ loves the church—in a selfless, sacrificial manner (Eph. 5:25). Husbands are to love their wives as they love their own bodies (Eph. 5:28). These instructions of Paul must have sounded revolutionary in his day, coming into a culture that viewed men as dominant and of clearly more worth than women.

Family headship, as spoken of by Paul, must always be exercised with great concern for the other members of the family. The one representing the family must never let his or her interest become selfish or motivated by the desire to assume a more dominant position.

The second question is, Why does Paul attribute headship to the male? Historically, the answer to this question has gone in two different directions. One answer is that the male is designated head because of creation; that is, this is the way God intended it from the beginning. For those holding to this view, "male headship" is to be maintained because that is the divine creation order. They find support for their interpretation in Genesis 1 and 2 as well as in their interpretation of certain Pauline references to the creation of man.

A second answer is that the male holds an authoritarian headship role primarily as the result of the Fall. An original relationship of complementarity and equality was perverted into one of dominance and subordination, because when man lost his proper relationship to God, there were effects in all his other relationships. However, those who hold this view can take either of two very different attitudes toward this concept of male dominance. The first is that male dominance in the headship role is the result of the curse and will remain throughout this present age; there is nothing we can do about it, for it will become radically different only in the eternal state, where all social relationships will take on a new and very different character. The second possible attitude is that when a person is reconciled to God through Christ, there is also a partial reconcilitation or healing of all those relationships which were broken by the original act of disobedience. In other words, after one becomes a "new person in Christ," the effects of the curse are continually lessened as one grows in Christ. Consequently, the pre-Fall relationship between husband and wife can be partially regained in our present world, and that should be our goal. So those who think that male dominance is the result of the curse can hold very different ideas of its continuing inevitability in the lives of Christians.

A third view of Paul's attributing hardship to the male is also possible. Although it includes elements of both of the other views, it is more closely related in some ways to the former. It emphasizes three aspects of the creation narrative: (1) the essential equality of males and females, (2) their complementarity and organic unity, and (3) their created reproductive differences. These reproductive differences enable them to perform different tasks with different levels of skill. This in turn results in a division of labor that is observable today in nonmodern societies. In this division of labor, the male performs those tasks that require the greater physical strength, the greater amount of geographical mobility, and the more constant attention or attention at unpredictable times. The female, limited by the reproductive functions of pregnancy and nursing, performs those tasks that center on care of the home and children as well as those broader economic tasks that can be accomplished in conjunction with her domestic responsibilities (e.g., some forms of gathering and horticulture). Therefore the male, because of his greater potential for physical strength, his greater freedom to be away from home and children, and hence his greater ability to devote undivided attention to the tasks he takes on, tends to be assigned tasks like hunting, warfare, and government. This division of labor between the sexes can hardly be called the "creation order," inasmuch as it was not given to the first man as the God-ordained, timeless pattern for the allocation of societal tasks. However, it can be considered a logical outgrowth or derivation of the reproductive differences between females and males that are a part of their creation. Because the reproductive differences between the sexes lead to a division of tasks, there also arises a difference in decision-making responsibilities. The male, in his role of representing the family to the broader society, finds himself with a wider area of decision-making responsibility than the female. He is more involved in decisions that affect his family relative to other social units in society, while her decision making is more focused on domestic activities.

A common error is to extend the concept of male headship to a type of decision-making authority that sets the male up as the final authority in the family. That form of authority appears to be foreign to the creation narrative. The type of male headship that would normally have developed from God's creation became radically distorted by sin. The male took his wider range of tasks and associated decision-making responsibilities and used them as a beachhead to expand his authority into areas not justifiably his and to exercise his authority selfishly.

One major problem for interpreters of the Bible has been Paul's references to Genesis 1 and 2, which speak of males and females in a way that appears to be foreign to the creation account. For instance, in 1 Corinthians 11:1-15 Paul seems to suggest, on the basis of Genesis 2, that there is a hierarchical relationship between males and females; but when we examine Genesis 2, such an idea does not appear to be there at all.

These statements by Paul can be understood in several ways. First, one can say that Paul is reading into the creation account certain cultural or rabbinic interpretations that are foreign to it. This interpretation would emphasize that when Paul was converted he did not leave behind all his old Jewish and otherwise culturally tinged conceptions; some of them continued to infect his thinking. Another way of handling these Pauline passages is to claim that Paul understood the creation account better than we are able to, and that our inability to see there what Paul sees merely indicates his greater exegetical prowess.

Neither of these explanations is fully satisfactory. To claim that Paul's thinking in the New Testament still contains significant elements of non-Christian thinking undermines the trustworthiness of much of the New Testament; and to claim that the Old Testament contains a viewpoint that we cannot detect undermines our confidence in our ability to understand what Scripture says.

But there is still another view. It is that in these passages Paul is speaking not of the original creation order as given in Genesis 1 and 2 but rather of the pattern of task allocation between males and females that is the result of their created reproductive differences. Consequently, it would be very possible and very legitimate for Paul to refer to the creation account to support a position for the male that involves a headship function, that is, the function of representing the family unit in society. A division of tasks is an inevitable development in any society. Paul's central thrust in these passages, then, is not that man is superior to woman and that women are consequently to be subordinate and submissive; it is, rather, that those who by virtue of their social role have wider areas of task responsibility are not to use their position to exploit and misuse those with more restricted areas of responsibility, and that those with more restricted areas should not be insubordinate but should be supportive of those with wider areas.

The third question that remains to be answered is: In

what sphere(s) of activity is male headship a legitimate functional principle—the family, the church, or the larger society? Probably the two most common positions on this question are (1) in all of them and (2) in none of them. The early reformers held the first position;[14] contemporary Christian feminists generally hold the second.[15] But there are other possible positions. For example, one could accept the idea of male headship in the family but reject it with respect to the church and to the larger society.[16] (It is true that the two passages in the New Testament that bring the concept of head to the male-female relationship speak only of the husband-wife relationship.) But to deal with this question takes us beyond the scope of our study, which focuses on sex roles in relation to the family. The question of the role of women in the church (and of women's ordination) will not be answered here either explicitly or implicitly.

It is no secret that there is tension in the evangelical Christian community today regarding the roles of males and females in the family. The differences expressed are not primarily the result of different attitudes toward Scripture—a "higher" view as opposed to a "lower" view. Nor do these differences stem from different ways of interpreting Scripture—a "new" hermeneutic as opposed to an "old" hermeneutic. Nor are they the result of certain contemporary religious trends—"evangelicals" as opposed to "neo-evangelicals."

The tension we feel today regarding the biblically appropriate roles for adult females and males in the family is the result of a tension that is present in Scripture itself. In the first-century church, Paul and the other apostles were confronted with those who were defending the "old" way (established cultural customs regarding male-female relationships, master-slave relationships, and the like) and those who were advocating the "new" way (the apparent irrelevance of such customs because in Christ the human differences on which those customs were based are not significant). As Krister Stendahl says: "When Paul fought those who defended the old—as in Galatia—his bold vision of the new expressed itself most strongly as in Galatians 3:28. When he discerned the overstatement of the new he spoke up for the old, as in Corinthians."[17]

To preserve unity in the body of Christ at that time, Paul had to temper the positions of such opposing elements in the church. Stendahl concludes: "Our problem is not to harmonize the two tendencies into a perfect system. It is—as always in a truly Christian theology—to discern where the accent should lie now, the accent in the eschatological drama which we call the history of the church and the world."[18] No amount of biblical exegesis and discussion will result in a final resolution of this tension. At best, we can hope that such efforts will ease the tension and make the issue more manageable in our present cultural situation.

In Galatians 3, the Apostle Paul gives a vision of the nature of the new Christian community. The most immediate implementation of that vision was the overcoming of the distinction between "Jew and Greek" (v. 28) in the first-century church. There was tension, of course, but the vision was implemented at that stage. Many hundreds of years passed before that vision could be implemented with respect to "slave and freeman." Again there was tension; in the United States it resulted in a civil war. Yet finally this stage of the vision was implemented, and the church became stronger because of it. But the vision was not yet complete. Now the tension focuses on "male and female." As before, the tension will result in an implementation of the vision at yet another level.

First-century Christian practices are not automatically to be considered the intended standard for the church at all ages. It is a denial of the dynamic nature of the Kingdom of God to make first-century practices—such as wearing veils and greeting one another with a holy kiss—into norms if the reason for doing so is solely that they were done in the first century. A cultural practice must at all times be judged by whether it expresses the will of God in the appropriate way for that time and place. We are not to play "First Century" but must seek to play, in a biblically normative way, "Twentieth Century." Stendahl's warning is appropriate: "If the actual stage of implementation in the first century becomes the standard for what is authoritative, then those elements which point toward future implementation become neutralized and absorbed in a static 'biblical view.'" [19]

Too many exegetical questions remain unanswered—and perhaps will never be answered—for us to attempt to prescribe a final, detailed solution. Nevertheless, the central message of Scripture for the male-female relationship in marriage is clear. Any resolution of the tension surrounding contemporary sex roles in the family must recognize that the Bible teaches: (1) the essential equality of women and men, (2) the complementarity or organic unity of husbands and wives, and (3) a differentiation of roles between wives and husbands that is based on their created reproductive differences.

The question now becomes: What are the implications of this biblical message for the contemporary sex-role issue in American society?

A Biblical Critique of the Traditional Female Role

The fundamental tasks of the traditional female role in American society are rearing children and taking care of the home. Although, as we saw in chapter 5, both women and society at large pay a high price for the limiting of women to these tasks, many Christians remain convinced that this is the way things should be. They argue that although it is unfortunate that women have been discriminated against and limited in their participation in society, still the Bible clearly teaches that women ought to be restricted to the traditional domestic tasks of child rearing and household care.

These Christians support their position in two ways. First, they point out that by far the most common social role played by women in biblical times was a domestic one. Second, they quote those passages from the Bible that seem most clearly to attach child care and household duties to women, such as: "So I counsel younger widows to marry, to have children, to manage their homes and to give the enemy no opportunity for slander" (1 Tim. 5:14); and, "the older women . . . can train the younger women to love their husbands and children . . . to be busy at home . . . to be subject to their husbands, so that no one will malign the word of God" (Titus 2:3-5).

The fact that women in biblical times were characteristically limited to child rearing and household tasks is certainly not enough to recommend this pattern as normative for today. To say that it *is* enough is to use Scripture inappropriately by failing to recognize that the Bible was written in a particular historical context. Certainly Scripture indicates that the primary social tasks ascribed to women in biblical times were child rearing and household care. As we have seen, women in all nonmodern societies had more pregnancies and a shorter life expectancy than women in modern America. They also had to nurse their babies, something not necessarily required of women today.

A knowledge of the historical context in which Paul wrote helps to reveal that in 1 Timothy 5:14 and Titus 2:3-5 he is not limiting women to domestic duties for all time; rather, he is dealing with a problem he frequently faced in attempting to spread the gospel. Women in Paul's day lived in patriarchal societies and were commonly thought of as second-class citizens. Biblical scholar Gerhard Kittel maintains that women's status in New Testament times is summarized well by a saying prevalent in one form or another in many societies of that day: men gave thanks that they were not unbelievers, uncivilized men, slaves, or women.[20] A particularly low estimation of women's capabilities and status was found in Judaism at that time.[21] Jewish religious and family life was male-dominated. Only the male was obligated to keep the whole Torah. Women were not permitted to learn the Torah, nor were they believed fit to witness, to instruct children, or to pray at meals. A wife was expected to sacrifice liberally for the benefit of her husband and subject herself fully to his will.

In this strongly patriarchal, highly restrictive social atmosphere, the message of Jesus Christ surely sounded both radical and liberating to women. All people—males, females, Greeks, Jews—were to be joint heirs in redemption (Rom. 8:14-17; 1 Peter 2:9; Gal. 3:26-28). Jesus' behavior also revealed a new attitude toward women in the redemptive order. He openly taught women (Luke 10:38-42; Luke 21:1-4; John 4:7-29), and both publicly touched them (Luke 13:10-13) and permitted Himself to be touched by them (Mark 5:25-34). Such acts were directly contrary to Jewish norms and signaled a new freedom and status for women under Christianity. Theologian Paul K. Jewett forcefully sums up Jesus' relationship to women in these words:

> It was not so much in what he said as in how he related to women that Jesus was a revolutionary. In this relationship his life style was so remarkable that one can only call it astonishing. He treated women as fully human, equal to men in every respect; no word of deprecation about women, as such, is ever found on his lips.[22]

This new freedom for women under the gospel of Jesus Christ was not understood by those outside the church. To them, Christianity was a radical belief system, judging from its view of women. In addition, some Christian women were abusing their new-found freedom. Some in Corinth, for instance, apparently were disrupting church services with much the same idle talk and gossip of which the widows in 1 Timothy 5:11-15 are accused.[23] Paul's response to this situation was to call Christian women to order. They, like other Christians, were not to flout the customs of the day. Such behavior would alienate non-Christians from the Christian community and the message of the gospel.

In 1 Timothy 5:14 and Titus 2:3-5, then, Paul is not limiting women for all time to the tasks of child rearing and household care. Instead, he is admonishing these women to respect certain cultural patterns of their day so that "no one will malign the word of God" (Titus 2:5), or "give the enemy . . . opportunity for slander" (1 Tim. 5:14). Observing certain cultural patterns in order that Christians will not be perceived as socially disruptive and thus hinder the spread of the gospel is a principle on which Paul frequently rests his teachings. He states it most explicitly in 1 Corinthians 10:31-33. This is the same principle that Paul invokes (in the same Titus 2 passage) when instructing slaves to obey their masters in all respects (2:9-10).

Given the principle underlying Paul's admonitions in 1 Timothy 5:14 and Titus 2:3-5, one might well argue that in our present cultural situation, with its greater emphasis on "liberating" women, the spread of the gospel might best be served by a Christian community that encourages and supports women who wish to engage in social activities outside the confines of the traditional female role.

Other passages in the Bible also indicate that women are not to be restricted to their traditional domestic role. In the Old Testament, Miriam is spoken of as a prophetess and leader (Exod. 15:20), Deborah as a judge and prophetess (Judg. 4:4-5), Huldah as a prophetess (2 Kings

22:14), and Esther as a queen who averted the destruction of her people. The New Testament records that Anna was a prophetess (Luke 2:36), that Lydia was in business selling purple dye (Acts 16:14), that Philip had four daughters who were prophetesses (Acts 21:9), and that Priscilla and several other women were fellow workers with Paul in spreading the gospel (Rom. 16:1-16). The manner in which these women are written about in the Bible suggests that they and their nondomestic activities were a credit to God and the covenant community.

The most explicit statement in Scripture about not limiting women to the traditional female role is contained in Proverbs 31, where the capable or ideal wife is described. She does not restrict her activities to child care and household tasks but is involved in every phase of administering a large estate. She organizes the activities of her servants. After careful consideration she purchases a plot of land for a vineyard and finances the planting of it with money she has earned. She works at meeting the needs of the poor. She weaves and sells linen, and supplies merchants with sashes. These administrative and business activities are presented not as mere appendages to the domestic tasks spoken of in this passage but as activities integral to the role of the ideal wife.

In addition to not restricting women to domestic tasks, Scripture does not define as women's work that which traditionally has been cited as the most important female task—child rearing. Nowhere does the Bible teach that women should be primarily responsible for the rearing of children. Rather the command to bring up children according to God's norms is given generally, to both parents (Gen. 18:19; Deut. 6:6-7; 11:19; Prov. 22:6; Eph. 6:4). Furthermore, the command given to children is to obey fathers and mothers (Exod. 20:12; Eph. 6:1-3; Col. 3:20), which suggests that both parents are responsible for rearing their children.

In view of the biblical evidence, then, what should Christians say about woman's role in modern society? We have seen that (1) Scripture does not teach that certain tasks must be ascribed to females, (2) there are apparently no God-created biological differences between the sexes that would limit women to certain tasks in modern society, and (3) research evidence clearly indicates that numerous negative social consequences for women result from traditional patterns of female sex-role socialization. Therefore Christians should be advocates of a sex-role structure that allows women full opportunity to develop their God-given gifts. Christians should emphasize the biblical norm of stewardship of talents (Luke 12:35-48; 16:1-13; 1 Cor. 4:2) instead of continuing to support the traditional female role with its artificial ascription of tasks and the associated forms of discrimination.

A Biblical Critique of the Traditional Male Role

The basic components of the traditional male role in American society are being an aggressive, competitive provider for the family and being the "head of the house," that is, the family's primary decision maker. Biblically, this conception is lacking in a number of respects.

First, it was pointed out earlier that Scripture commands parents to take joint responsibility for rearing their children according to God's norms. Given the present sex-role structure, this is very difficult for a Christian husband to do. Much more so than in our agrarian past, males as providers are required to be away from home during the day. And in the evenings they are often away at community and church meetings, since society has been reluctant to give women leadership roles in the community and church. Thus the father's socializing influence upon his children is often reduced to that of an "enforcer"—the mother, when at a loss to control the children, threatens them by saying, "Just wait until your father gets home!" Such a situation hardly complies with the scriptural directives on child rearing.

Second, in the Bible the task of family providing is not assigned only—or even primarily—to the husband. According to Proverbs 31, the ideal wife is very much involved in this task. Elsewhere Scripture indicates that providing for the family is a parental function rather than a task assigned to either the husband or wife (2 Cor. 12:14). The sort of family providing that either the husband or the wife does in a nonmodern society is affected by the reproductive differences between the sexes, but, as we saw in chapter 3, women have taken on a major share of this family task in most human societies.

A third biblically based criticism of the traditional male role centers on the cultural belief that it is the husband's right and responsibility to make decisions for the family—he is the "head of the house." This belief places the wife in a subordinate position to her husband. In the past, the husband's dominant position was represented in laws that gave him the right to control his wife's body and property. Although this inequality of the sexes before the law has fast been disappearing in modern society, traditional patterns of socialization still emphasize that the final authority in the family resides with the husband.

It is clear from our earlier discussion of the relationship of males and females in Creation, in the Fall, and in redemption that such a conception of male authority is without scriptural basis. That the male is the final authority in the marriage relationship is an idea that is foreign to the Bible. Paul does speak of husbands as possessing a headship or representative role in the family, but this is a functional role that fell to husbands because of two factors: the created reproductive differences between men and women, and the conditions under which people lived in nonmodern societies.

Moreover, to recognize that the husband took on a

wider range of decision-making responsibility because he was the family's representative to other social units is not to maintain that the husband was in authority over the wife. It is to state that the husband as "head" found himself with a wider range of decision-making responsibility because that responsibility accompanied the task of family representative; if the husband was absent or incapacitated, undoubtedly the wife took on that role of headship. Neither Paul nor the creation account in Genesis 1 and 2 grants the male the final authority in the marriage relationship for all time. Such a notion of a "final authority" in marriage must be seen as a perverted view of headship, one that resulted from the Fall. The vision of Scripture for the marriage relationship is one of female-male equality and complementarity—a relationship of organic unity in which husband and wife render selfless service to each other.

It is not easy for modern Americans to understand what Paul was emphasizing with this metaphor of headship. First, we come to this passage with a cultural heritage that includes the man as "the head of the house." To most Americans, the head is the one who has the "say-so" in marriage; but to Paul, headship suggested the role of family representative within the "one flesh" or organically unified marriage relationship as laid down in Genesis 1 and 2. In addition, thinking about social organization in terms of that organic model instead of a hierarchical one is foreign to most Americans. Churches, schools, businesses, government, the military—all are hierarchically organized into layers of decision-making authority. One does not see any groups or organizations structured primarily according to mutual subjection, love, and respect. It is not surprising, then, that among the first questions Americans have about the marriage relationship is, Who has the final word? Yet the emphasis of Paul and of Genesis 1 and 2 on an organic model for marriage relationships is more consistent with what Christ said about all social relationships. Christ made it clear in His teachings that questions of power or final authority were not the important questions to ask about social relationships. Instead He taught His disciples something that is as foreign to our time as it was to theirs:

> 25 "You know that the rulers of the Gentiles lord it over them, and their high officials exercise authority over them. 26Not so with you. Instead, whoever wants to become great among you must be your servant, 27and whoever wants to be first must be your slave— 28just as the Son of Man did not come to be served, but to serve, and to give his life a ransom for many" (Matt. 20:25-28).

Christians, then, must first of all be concerned with serving one another.

In practice, this dominant message of the Christian gospel for the marriage relationship makes largely irrelevant our preoccupation with this question: In the case of an impasse, who has the right to make the final decision? If the marital partners truly attempt to practice mutual servanthood, subjection, love, and respect, impasses are unlikely to occur. If a supposedly unresolvable difference arises, it is usually because the partners (or perhaps one of the two) are unwilling to be "slaves" to one another out of obedience to Christ.

The implications of this biblical evidence for the traditional male role in American society are apparent. The Christian who accepts the biblical model of equality and complementarity for marriage cannot at the same time accept a traditional male role that views the husband as "the head of the house" in the sense of being the final authority in the family. Moreover, it should also be recognized that the male headship (representative) role that Paul speaks of is becoming less and less of a functional necessity in American society as women's social participation becomes less limited by their reproductive role.

So far, this biblically based critique of the traditional

male role has focused on the tasks included in the male role. We have argued that assigning family providing and family decision making exclusively to the husband is without scriptural basis. But there is still one other respect in which the traditional male role is biblically lacking: American society's conception of appropriate male role attributes.

The male in American society is encouraged to build his identity around a set of traits collectively known as "machismo." Machismo, or assertive masculinity, includes the attributes of being aggressive, competitive, tough, courageous, strong, unemotional, cool under pressure, and always in control. The male is expected to develop these traits within himself and then harness them in his quest for what is most valued in American society—individual success.

The way in which these male role attributes are expressed depends on what part of society one looks at. The young, unmarried, lower-class male tends to express these attributes in a physical fashion. Acceptance and status in his peer group depend largely upon physical prowess in fights and physical relationships with women that lack emotional attachment. The National Commission on the Causes and Prevention of Violence, after pointing out that the United States is a world leader in the violent crimes of rape, robbery, murder, and assault and that the main perpetrators of these crimes are lower-class males between the ages of fifteen and twenty-four, puts much of the blame for this on male role attributes: "Proving masculinity may require frequent rehearsals of toughness, the exploitation of women, and quick, aggressive responses." [24]

Although not nearly so likely to be acted out physically, male role attributes are thought to be equally important to the middle-class husband. In his role of family provider he is expected to strive for and eventually achieve economic success. Economic success in our highly competitive society, it is often argued, necessitates the masculine traits of being aggressive, often unemotional, coolly analytical, in control, and frequently manipulative of others. That many Americans have internalized these attributes to the extreme is reflected by the fact that Robert Ringer's book *Winning Through Intimidation* and Michael Korda's *Power! How to Get It, How to Use It* spent months on the *Publisher's Weekly* bestseller list. A *Time* magazine review of these books describes them as "psychic Charles Atlas courses" containing tips on how to succeed through the use of power, intimidation, and manipulation. Both books are based on this assumption: winning (economically) is what counts, and since others are out to take you for what they can get, you had better learn how to take care of yourself. According to Ringer, taking care of yourself means putting into practice principles like the "Ice Ball Theory," staying cool and unaffected in the face of great economic loss, and the "Theory of Intimidation," manipulating business situations so that those with whom you deal feel weaker, more vulnerable, and inferior to you.[25]

No matter how expressed, these male role attributes (aggressiveness, competitiveness, and the like), which even Christians often unthinkingly teach to boys, are not the attributes that Scripture instructs Christian men to exhibit. Paul says in Galatians 5:20-21 that Christians may not be characterized by "hatred, discord, jealousy, fits of rage, selfish ambition, dissensions, factions, and envy." Instead, they are to bear "the fruit of the Spirit . . . love, joy, peace, patience, kindness, goodness, faithfulness, gentleness and self-control. Against such things there is no law. Those who belong to Christ Jesus have crucified their sinful nature with its passions and desires. Since we live by the Spirit, let us keep in step with the Spirit" (Gal. 5:22-25). The traditional male role attributes differ markedly from Paul's description.

Toward a More Christian
Sex-Role Structure

It has been argued here that the traditional sex-role structure in American society that has designated "appropriate behaviors" for women and men in the context of the family is subject to biblical criticism on a number of counts. First, society has ascribed tasks to females in such a limited fashion that women have been discriminated against and many of their God-given gifts have been wasted. Second, practicing the traditional male role makes it difficult for Christian men today to take an active part in their biblically based child-rearing responsibilities. Third, the male role ascribes to men a type of decision-making authority that is unscriptural. Finally, traditional male role attributes appear to be at odds with biblical teaching.

These criticisms suggest a more Christian orientation toward both the task component and the attribute component of sex roles. First, regarding sex-role tasks: since Scripture does not normatively teach that child rearing and care of the home are to be ascribed to women only, or family providing and decision making to men only, and because Scripture does teach that we are to be good stewards of our gifts in our role of Christian servanthood to others, we in the Christian community should emphasize flexibility in how tasks are divided between the sexes. The norm guiding the division of labor in the family should be stewardship of God-given talents, not ascription by sex. Without a biological basis for sex roles, modern American society has great potential for such task flexibility and stewardship of talents.

We must be careful of sex-role ideologies that initially appear to have a message of tolerance but turn out to be as limiting in their own ways as the traditional sex roles. A good example of exchanging one form of intolerance and limitation for another under the guise of radical change can be seen in a dialogue between the moderate feminist Betty Friedan and the radical feminist Simone de Beauvoir.[26] At one point in the dialogue, Friedan asks de Beauvoir if she thinks certain women ought to be permitted the option of home without career if these women are convinced that this would be in the best interests of themselves and their families. De Beauvoir's answer is no, because she feels too many women would make that choice. The implication is that society has so warped women through the socialization process that they *think* they want the traditional female role when really they do not. Therefore, suggests de Beauvoir, women must be required to accept nontraditional roles. This vision that de Beauvoir holds for the future is as limiting and as contradictory to a more complete stewardship of gifts as the sex-role limitations of the past.

The sort of task flexibility advocated here requires that prior to marriage, a couple discuss how they as a partnership will accomplish fundamental family tasks like providing and child rearing. It means that in family decision making, husband and wife will act as partners, paying attention to each other's background knowledge and experience in relation to the particular decision at hand. And it means that the family, the church, and the school as agencies of socialization will stop sex-typing tasks. For Christians, the point here is that, regardless of sex, they ought to work to develop their individual talents so that they can be more responsible servants in God's kingdom.

The second component of roles is role attributes. Christians, like non-Christians, have generally felt that men and women should have different sets of attributes. An example is an advertisement for courses on "Teaching Boys to be Manly for Christ" and "Teaching Girls to be Lovely for Christ." But if one examines the Bible, only one set of attributes is presented as significant—the fruit of the Spirit. Paul instructs Christians in Galatians 5 to be loving, faithful, patient, kind, and gentle. Christ's Sermon on the Mount (Matt. 5–7) and Paul's description of Christian behavior in Romans 12 emphasize the same qualities. Neither Christ nor Paul sex-types the characteristics for which Christians are to strive, nor does either suggest that the sexes should have different attributes. In view of all this, Christians should not socialize their children into a "masculine" or a "feminine" identity that is stereotypic and hence limiting but should try to instill a *Christian* identity based on the fruits of the Spirit.

In urging that the Christian community move more toward task flexibility and toward identities based on Christian attributes regardless of sex, we may give some the impression that we are advocating some kind of unisex Christian community. That is not the intention. Society currently encourages people to base their general identities as women or men on two more specific, distinguishable identities. One of these is a "gender" identity composed of the tasks and attributes attached to traditional sex roles. The other is a "sexual" identity based on differences of anatomy, reproductive functions, and sexual response. Gender identities are a matter of social definition, and much of their content is at odds with fundamental biblical norms; sexual identities, on the other hand, are based on God-created biological differences and thus are part of the created order. What is being advocated here is the removal of traditional gender identities; sexual identities will always remain.

God created people as male and female, and men and women will always recognize this difference and relate to each other in terms of it. But adding to the God-created difference between male and female by artificially ascribing certain social tasks and attributes to one sex or the other does nothing to enhance that difference. What it does is limit individual potential.

Discussion Questions

1/ Christians in the first century experienced tensions over the Jew-Greek, male-female, and slave-freeman distinctions. To what extent are the social tensions in the Christian community today the result of the same distinctions among people? Are there additional differences among people that today are producing tensions in social relationships?

2/ What can we do to overcome these sources of tension among Christians and to achieve the unity that should characterize the Christian church?

3/ To what extent are your ideas of male and female roles derived from Scripture and to what extent are they derived from your culture?

4/ If Christ's work in redemption has a restorative effect on human relationships, how do you think this restoration ought to be expressed in our families and our churches?

5/ Do you think the current dating system reinforces traditional sex roles? If so, how? Would another kind of dating system be more consistent with the redemptive vision for the male-female relationship?

6/ Can you think of an example of an impasse in marriage that the partners could not resolve by practicing mutual Christian servanthood?

7/ What sorts of things could a church do to encourage a more flexible view of sex roles? What could the school do? The family?

Suggested Readings

De Boer, Willis P. "Calvin on the Role of Women." In *Exploring the Heritage of John Calvin,* edited by David E. Holwerda, pp. 236-72. Grand Rapids: Baker Book House, 1976.

A well-documented analysis of what Calvin thought about women, showing how his view was the product both of his understanding of Scripture and of the culture in which he lived.

Jewett, Paul King. **Man as Male and Female.** Grand Rapids: William B. Eerdmans Publishing Co., 1975.

A study of male-female relationships from a theological point of view. The author, a professor of systematic theology at Fuller Seminary, basically worked from an evangelical perspective. However, he used a somewhat nontraditional approach to biblical interpretation and arrived at a number of nontraditional conclusions. Evangelicals will find the book both instructive and disturbing.

Stendahl, Krister, **The Bible and the Role of Women.** Philadelphia: Fortress Press, 1966.

The author, who represents a fairly liberal theological orientation, has written this small book (48 pages) as a case study in biblical interpretation. The conclusions are basically in accord with those of the Christian feminist movement. Although many evangelicals will take issue with Stendahl, all will find this study very thought-provoking.

/7/

SOME IMPLICATIONS OF A MORE CHRIS-TIAN SEX-ROLE STRUCTURE

In the first chapter of this book we discussed some long-range technological and social changes that are affecting the family. These and the contemporary feminist movement have converged to produce more participation by women in paid employment and a general blurring of the roles traditionally played by men and women. These trends give rise to some questions that are very troublesome to many Christians, mainly: What is the impact on the family of married women's increased participation in the labor force? And, how acceptable are the primary goals of the mainline feminist movement?

Working Married Women:
The Issues

As recently as 1940, only 15 percent of married women held jobs; today well over 40 percent do. The employment rate for married women with children ages six through seventeen has more than quintupled from an estimated 9 percent in 1940 to 52 percent in 1975. The rate for married women with children under six has risen significantly, too—from 13 percent in 1950 to 37 percent in 1975.

As this trend was developing in the late forties and the fifties, ministers, legislators, judges, and others began to blame many of society's ills on working mothers. They were thought to contribute to the increase in juvenile delinquency and divorce. Although perhaps less commonly than in the past, Christians today are making some similar claims. States one writer in a Christian periodical:

> One of the saddest cases in our own community involved a teenager arrested on a serious charge and turned over to a social worker for counseling. His mother had taken a job as a professional social worker. What this mother was doing for money she had failed to do for love. Now another social worker had to be found to counsel her son.[1]

In a more general vein, the same person writes:

> If a woman is involved all day long in doing something that has no relation to her family, it may be difficult for her to switch roles at the end of the day. She is likely to be preoccupied and tired, to feel more like being served than serving. There are bound to be consequences for husbands and children. There is no territorial imperative cited in Scripture that says a woman's place is unalterably in the house. But especially today Christian families ought to be thinking how the father, mother, and children can spend more time together rather than less.[2]

Aside from the questionable assumptions about the appropriate responsibilities of Christian husbands and wives, these quotations do raise legitimate questions about the consequences for the family of women's move into nontraditional roles. Those of us in the Christian community who are arguing for less rigidity in sex roles must address these questions. If it can be shown that the employment of married women has serious negative consequences for the various members of the family, then other ways will have to be found to bring about a greater flexibility in task assignment and stewardship of talents for women and men.

What then are the consequences when married women work outside the home? Fortunately, society's substantial criticism of this practice after World War II prompted a considerable amount of research into its effects.[3]

The Consequences for the Child. Do the children of working mothers perform more poorly in school than those of nonworking mothers? Is maternal employment related to juvenile delinquency? Does it affect the mental stability of children?

Research does not show sizable differences in academic performance between the children of working mothers and the children of nonworking mothers. Certain studies have shown a slight but not significant tendency for the children of working mothers in the middle class to obtain higher grades, but the opposite appears true in the lower class. Given the present state of research, these can be accepted only as very tentative conclusions.

It has often been argued that because working mothers are absent from the home more than nonworking mothers, their children are less supervised and hence more prone to delinquency. The data do not bear out this argument. As with academic achievement, there are small differences by social class. Sons of working mothers in the middle class appear to be slightly more delinquent than sons of nonworking mothers, but in the lower class there is no difference. The lack of significant differences here is understandable when one considers the fact that children old enough to commit delinquent acts are already of school age. If their mothers are employed, those mothers are likely to be working while the children are under the supervision of school personnel.

People reared in American society, where the traditional pattern has been for infants and young children to be cared for primarily by a single maternal figure, are likely to think that alternatives to this pattern may well damage a child's emotional development, even to the point of precipitating mental illness. Those who think this are not without their professional supporters.[4] Yet family sociologists Nye and Berardo state, "None of the current research found any measurable differences in symptoms of poor mental health in the children of employed and nonemployed mothers."[5] What seem to be crucial for the mental development of a child are such things as warmth, affection, stimulation, and adequate food. In other words, the data suggest that the more important factor here is quality of care, not who performs that care.

Another concern about working mothers is the effect on the mother's emotional state and hence on her adequacy as a mother when she does have contact with her children. It has been suggested that working outside the home may drain the mother physically and emotionally to the extent that she has little left to give to her children when she does return home.

Research, however, finds a number of mediating factors. One is whether or not a woman is satisfied with her lot of working or not working. Researchers studying mothers of elementary school children divided the women into four groups: satisfied working mothers, dissatisfied working mothers, satisfied nonworking mothers, and dissatisfied nonworking mothers. On a scale designed to measure adequacy of mothering, satisfied nonworking women scored the highest, dissatisfied nonworking women the lowest, while the two categories of working women fell in between. Since satisfied working women scored lower on adequate parenting than satisfied nonworking women but higher than dissatisfied nonworking women, the crucial question becomes: Would a working mother who enjoys her occupation be dissatisfied as a full-time homemaker? The answer appears to be yes.[6] Data on professionally employed mothers and mothers who graduated from college with exceptionally high records but had chosen to become full-time homemakers showed that the homemakers in this case were lower in morale, self-esteem, and feelings of personal competence (even in regard to child rearing) and showed a greater concern about personal-identity issues. When questioned about what they felt was most notably absent from their lives, the professional women responded that they lacked "time"; the full-time homemakers most often mentioned the lack of "challenge and creative involvement."

Another mediating factor is the extent to which the working mother feels guilty for not being a full-time housewife-mother. There is evidence that employed women do feel guilty about being absent from home. Even the relatively happy professional women in the research just mentioned indicated that they frequently felt anxious and guilty about their employment and its effects on their children. This is hardly surprising in a society that has traditionally looked askance at working mothers. The implications of these feelings of anxiety for the children of working mothers are not fully known. But if any reasonably clear pattern has emerged from the research in this area, it is that mothers who feel very guilty about working tend to overcompensate by being overindulgent and overprotective toward their children.[7] As it becomes more and more culturally acceptable for mothers to work, the guilt feelings and their results are likely to diminish.

One last mediating factor involved in the mother's emotional state is the degree of role strain she experiences. Common sense would have it that working part-time may place little strain on a mother and indirectly her children but working full-time creates a lot more strain and more adverse effects. Research evidence simply does not permit this blanket contention. What appears to be crucial here is whether or not the woman feels her child-care and household-care arrangements are adequate, not whether she works full- or part-time. If she feels that the arrangements are acceptable, strain is minimized, and her emotional state and indirectly her children are not threatened by this source of anxiety.

In summarizing the evidence on the effect of working on a mother's emotional state, Lois Wladis Hoffman, an acknowledged expert in this area, states: "The working mother who obtains satisfaction from her work, who has adequate arrangements so that her dual role does not involve undue strain, and who does not feel so guilty that she overcompensates is likely to do quite well and, under certain conditions, better than the non-working mother."[8] Moreover, for mothers who wish to work, "the job often seems to act as a 'safety valve' . . . , reducing nervousness and frustration."[9]

A final area of research concerning the effects on children of a mother's employment has to do with the sort of role model she is presenting to them. Some are concerned that a working mother presents a role model that, because it is different from the one that mothers have traditionally presented, serves to confuse the children's role perceptions. They fear that such role ambiguity places undue strain on the child and hinders the child's identification with the parent.

Research does not substantiate such fears.[10] Boys in the middle class tend to identify with their fathers and accept them as role models as frequently when their mothers are employed as when they are not. However, this is not as true of sons in the lower class. A probable reason for this difference is that lower-class fathers are less frequently adequate providers and hence mothers are pressured to take jobs. Given present cultural values, in such cases it seems reasonable to presume that often someone other than the father who is inadequately providing would be selected as a role model.

Daughters at all social-class levels are more likely to select a mother who works as a role model than one who does not.[11] The reason why working mothers are more attractive role models to their daughters is so far an unresearched question. However, there has been considerable research on the consequences for daughters of having a working mother rather than a nonworking mother as a model, and from the perspective of moving toward a society more completely characterized by stewardship of talents and by task flexibility for women and men, those consequences are laudable.[12] For instance, research indicates that among girls of elementary school age, daughters of working mothers have a less stereotyped view of the world than daughters of nonworking mothers. The former were more likely to say that both men and women engage in a wide variety of activities, such as using guns, choosing home furnishings, and climbing mountains. The daughters of working women were also more likely to perceive women as being active in the world outside the home.

Another body of findings closely related to the idea of role modeling has to do with how the children of employed versus nonemployed women perceive role attributes for men and women. In a recent study of college-age students, the investigators found that children of both working and nonworking mothers tend to stereotype men as more competent and effective and women as more warm and expressive. However, this tendency was significantly more decided for the children of nonworking women. The authors conclude that maternal employment tends to soften sex-role stereotyping in children.[13]

Maternal employment also appears to have an effect on daughters' evaluation of female competence. In chapter 5 we looked at research by Goldberg in which he found that college women tended to view scholarly articles as less competently done if attributed to female rather than male authors. Later research, using the same research techniques but dividing the college women by the employment status of their mothers, found that the daughters of working women were much less likely to downgrade the competence of female authors than the daughters of nonworking women. Apparently, maternal employment helps daughters develop a more realistic view of the talents of women.

The Consequences for the Husband. A wife's employment has certain consequences for her husband and for their relationship. One of the more predictable ones is the effect on the division of labor in the home. As the wife moves into the provider role, the husband tends to get more involved in traditional female tasks. The evidence clearly shows that husbands of working women engage in more "homemaker tasks" like cleaning the house, caring for the children, doing dishes, and shopping for groceries than husbands of nonworking women. But they by no means come to share these tasks equally with their wives. Whether she works part-time or full-time, household care generally remains the wife's responsibility.

The relative contributions of husband and wife to family decision making are also affected by the wife's employment. Working wives have more influence than nonworking wives in decisions on such matters as borrowing money, paying bills, and determining what job the husband should take.[14] An important question about these findings is this: Do wives who were more influential in the first place tend to be the wives who get jobs, or does entering paid employment actually result in increased influence? Research comparing the influence of wives before and after employment indicates that the latter is more often the case. Generally speaking, if a wife enters the labor force, her husband can expect to share influence in the family decision-making process more than he did before.[15] This is hardly surprising, since she has now taken on an additional role that is highly valued in society. The change in the wife's influence is likely to be greater in the case of a lower-class than a middle-class family, because the lower-class family is usually less egalitarian to begin with.

A frequently recurring argument against the wife's employment involves the possible threat to the husband's ego. By moving into the traditionally accepted husband's domain of family providing, it is said, the wife may create feelings of inadequacy or hostility in the husband. There is not a great deal of evidence that husbands, at least at present, are particularly threatened by their wives' employment. The proportion of husbands who disapprove of their wives' work is very small and has been decreasing. The most common interpretation offered here is that husbands are not threatened because the jobs their wives hold are usually of lower status than their own.[16]

However, if the task flexibility and stewardship of talents argued for in the previous chapter becomes more of a reality, the status of working women will eventually become more comparable to that of their husbands. If this happens, traditionally oriented husbands may come to feel more threatened by their wives' employment. But the problem then for Christians will be not the wife's employment but the husband's response. If a husband feels inadequate because his wife shares in the responsibilities of family providing, he is basing his identity and establishing his self-worth on something other than the biblical attributes for Christians discussed in the previous chapter.

Marriages in which the wife works have more conflict between spouses than those in which the wife does not work. This holds true regardless of the family's size or social class or the educational level of the spouses. Although the difference in conflict level is not particularly large, it is significant enough that social scientists have tried to find out why it exists.[17]

They have advanced a number of possible explanations. One is that marriages involving working wives were more conflict-ridden to start with and this is what prompted wives to work. A second suggests that working wives, being less financially dependent on their husbands, are more likely to state their opinions when they disagree with their husbands and so contribute to a higher level of conflict. The third explanation is called the "increased interaction hypothesis." This maintains that with the wife-mother's employment, an additional dimension is added to the family's day-to-day life. The activities of all family members must be adjusted to the demands of the mother's job. This raises additional possibilities for disagreement and conflict. All three of these explanations have some empirical support and, depending on the family involved, can account for increased conflict in families with working wives.

A question closely allied to that of conflict in the marriages of working wives is whether the rise in the employment rate of wives has contributed to the increase in the divorce rate. While it is true that a disproportionate number of women who are divorced are also employed, it is common knowledge that many of these women work simply because for economic reasons they must. Comparisons of working and nonworking women reveal that a similar portion of each group were in their second or subsequent marriage. Although not definitive, this evidence does suggest that "it is more likely that divorced women get jobs than that women get divorces because they have jobs."[18]

There is one more facet to the relation between wives' employment and marital conflict. While it is true that working wives experience more conflict with their husbands than do nonworking wives, this does not mean that working wives are less satisfied with their marriages. The evidence is that they do not report any less satisfaction than nonworking wives. In fact, if they take jobs voluntarily, their satisfaction with marriage increases.[19] Apparently, if a wife enters the labor force because she wishes to, she can generally expect a higher standard of living, more influence in family decision making, and additional social relationships—that is, with people at her place of work. While her job tends to result in more conflict with her husband, it also adds satisfaction to her life. That satisfaction seemingly extends to her assessment of her marriage.

The Consequences for the Working Wife-Mother. When married women significantly increased their participation in the labor force after World War II, they were accused of possibly harming not only their children but also themselves. Although there has been less research in this area than into the consequences for children and the husband-wife relationship, there are enough data to dismiss some of the more common myths about working mothers.

One such myth is that taking on the additional role of paid employee negatively affects a mother's physical health. According to research evidence, employed mothers as a category apparently are healthier than nonemployed mothers;[20] they report considerably fewer symptoms of poor health. Whether working improves the health of the mother or healthier mothers tend to be the ones working is an unanswered question. Before-and-after research is needed in this area. At any rate, the finding that working mothers are generally healthier than nonworking mothers is sufficient reason to dismiss the assumption that employment is necessarily a detriment to the mother's physical health.

Although nonworking mothers also have doubts about

their adequacy as mothers and wives, more working mothers experience these doubts. The working mothers who are most subject to feelings of guilt and anxiety are those who are not satisfied with their substitute child-care arrangements and those whose own parents are very traditionally oriented toward the mother's role.

Working mothers' feelings of guilt and anxiety about their mother-wife roles, however, do not seem to get transferred into psychosomatic symptoms of mental illness. For instance, one major study measured ten psychosomatic symptoms, including shortness of breath, nightmares, nervousness, insomnia, and dizziness. No significant differences were found between working and nonworking mothers.[21] In fact, the minor differences were on the side of more symptoms among the nonworking mothers.

Perhaps part of the reason why working mothers' anxiety about how well they are fulfilling traditional female role expectations does not get transformed into psychosomatic symptoms is that working mothers tend to feel better about themselves than nonworking mothers. In studies of self-concept, working mothers are more likely to mention positive things about themselves and to show self-acceptance than nonworking mothers.[22]

Other consequences of employment for working married women are quite predictable. For instance, they spend less time at recreational pursuits. Interestingly, the recreational activities reduced are watching television, visiting neighbors, and entertaining formally. There is no reduction in recreation involving the husband or the family as a whole. Employed mothers are also less likely to take positions of responsibility in voluntary organizations, but they are as likely as nonemployed mothers to belong to such organizations and attend the meetings.

Much argument over married women's employment centers on whether it increases or decreases happiness.

Some argue that it brings fulfillment, others that it produces more conflict and tension in the family and hence unhappiness. Researcher F. Ivan Nye asked two thousand mothers to indicate the degree of their satisfaction or dissatisfaction with several areas of their lives.[23] These areas included such things as daily work, income, relationship with their children, and their community as a place to live. Overall, working mothers, whether employed part-time or full-time, showed more satisfaction with their lives than nonworking mothers. Interestingly, the differences between the two groups were greatest in two non-material areas: relationship with their children and how they viewed their community as a place to live. In both, working mothers were found to be more satisfied than nonworking mothers. Whatever the perceived costs of employment for working mothers, these costs do not appear sufficient to give the women a negative assessment of their lot in life. If anything, such women are more likely to feel positive about their lives.

Conclusion. From a sociological perspective, there do not appear to be significant negative social consequences associated with the employment of mothers and wives. Working mothers experience more feelings of guilt and anxiety about their adequacy as mothers, but this does not get transformed into negative consequences for their children. They also experience similar doubts regarding their adequacy as wives, but these feelings do not lead to greater dissatisfaction with their marriages or more symptoms of physical or mental illness. Nor does the greater amount of conflict in the marriages of working wives seem to result in higher divorce rates or less satisfaction with their marriages. All this is not to say that taking on an additional role is not difficult or does not create strain; what the evidence does suggest is that working women and their families have found ways to cope with that strain fairly effectively.[24]

From the point of view that it is desirable for society to move more toward sex-role task flexibility and less sex stereotyping of attributes so that stewardship of gifts can be more fully realized, the increased participation of married women in the labor force seems to have many positive consequences. Their children are less likely to stereotype roles for women and men. Their daughters evaluate the competence of women more highly. Their children and husbands share more in day-to-day household tasks. Their husbands are likely to share family decision making with them. And their self-images are higher.

Although extensive, the research about the consequences of married women's employment is not as complete as we would like. Of primary concern to Christian parents, for instance, is the spiritual growth of their children. With so many non-Christian influences at work in society, they are rightfully concerned with anything that might hinder this aspect of their children's development. Although the sociological evidence on married women's employment does not directly address this concern, it does indirectly offer some reassurance by suggesting that working mothers are as influential in their children's lives as nonworking mothers. Quality of child care appears more important than the absolute amount of time spent with the child or who offers the care. Children of working mothers identify with their parents as readily as children of nonworking mothers. Once employed, mothers do not reduce recreational time spent with their children. Working mothers are as satisfied with their relationship to their children as nonworking mothers.

In the end, it must be remembered that these sociological statements are generalizations, or statements of probability; they must not be indiscriminately applied to particular families. Decisions about how a given wife and husband will responsibly provide for their family must depend upon their particular situation. However, these generalizations surely should be sufficient to reassure the Christian community that the trend toward married women's employment has not ushered in the negative results for the family that were predicted. Throughout this section we have compared working and nonworking women in order to reach some conclusion about the consequences of women's taking on a share of the family providing role. Does this mean that if the consequences on balance had been found to be negative, we would be saying that responsible Christians ought to speak out against married women's employment? No. The way in which the issue was handled here was merely a reflection of the way in which previous social scientists have conceptualized the issue and collected relevant data. Regardless of whether the consequences proved to be decidedly negative or decidedly positive, the basic question for each Christian husband and wife would remain the same: how can they fulfill family responsibilities and at the same time make optimum use of their talents in their roles of Christian servanthood? Since each marriage represents a unique combination of talents and conditions, practicing such an orientation will mean that some Christian families look quite traditional in their structure for accomplishing family tasks while others appear non-traditional (e.g., husband and wife share equally in family providing and child rearing, or the wife as the primary provider and the husband the main child rearer).

Some Issues for Christians Arising From the Contemporary Feminist Movement

As noted in chapter 1, the contemporary feminist movement is made up of a diversity of organizations with a wide variation in goals. Extremist elements of the movement have advocated such things as the destruction of the nuclear family, the acceptability and value of lesbian relationships, and abortion on demand. In view of scriptural statements about marriage and parental responsibilities, the sinfulness of lesbian relationships (Rom. 1:26), and the importance of fetal life (Exod. 21:22-24; Ps. 139:16), evangelical Christians have had little difficulty in rejecting such goals. However, other goals of the feminist movement are not as easily discarded by quoting specific biblical passages. Two goals vigorously promoted by the reformist wing of the movement are government-supported day-care facilities and equal rights for women and men before the law. These demand careful and objective analysis by evangelical Christians.

Government-Supported Day Care. At certain points in this century, the government has provided day-care facilities for at least a short time. The primary impetus for this service was depression and war.[25] During the 1930s, day-care services were set up in association with the Works Progress Administration (WPA). Their purpose was to create employment for teachers, nutritionists, clerical workers, and maintenance people who were out of work because of the Depression. These workers were to serve children ages two through five who were from welfare families. By the early forties, WPA nurseries were no longer needed as a source of employment, and the federal government decided to withdraw its nursery services to welfare children. However, administrators were told that they could convert their facilities to wartime nurseries to care for the children of mothers needed in the war industries. These new day-care facilities were supported by funds appropriated under the Lanham Act, passed in 1941.

After World War II this service was withdrawn. Since that time the government has on rare occasions included some form of preschool child care as part of a larger social program—for example, Project Headstart for youngsters as part of the Economic Opportunity Act of 1964. Here again, the program was limited to a specific category of preschooler rather than being available to all young children.

Although the role of government in child care may be debatable, certain data suggest a growing need for day-care centers of some type. Among mothers of children six through seventeen, the proportion who hold jobs has increased from 9 percent in 1940 to 52 percent in 1975. For those with children under six, their participation rate has risen from 13 percent in 1950 to 37 percent in 1975. Yet licensed public and voluntary day-care centers service only one-sixth the number of children they serviced at the end of World War II.[26] The majority of the young children of working mothers are now cared for in their own homes by a sibling, a father, another relative, or a nonrelative. According to a study by the Office of Economic Opportunity, 55 percent of all children cared for outside their own homes go to "family day-care homes," that is, private homes in which an adult cares for one or more children. The other 45 percent go to day-care centers.[27] Although many more children of working mothers are cared for in their own homes or in family day-care homes than in day-care centers, this same study showed that mothers whose children were in day-care centers were the most satisfied with their child-care arrangements. This strongly suggests that there is a considerable need and demand for more day-care centers.

Other data also document the need for good day-care facilities.[28] It is estimated that at least 8 percent of the children of working mothers look after themselves. Of these, 4 percent are under the age of six. Moreover, in a Labor Department study of poor women who were unemployed but wanted to work, one-fifth cited the lack of adequate child care as the main reason why they were not looking for work. Finally, even in suburban areas where parents can afford to pay for day care, the demand far outstrips the supply.

In all likelihood, one reason why the United States lags behind many other modern nations in providing day care for young children is a strong cultural belief that a child's mother is the only really adequate agent of socialization in society. According to this thinking, if day care were more readily available, more mothers would work and more children would suffer the negative consequences of having a working mother.

The limited evidence summarized in the previous section does not seem to support this set of cultural beliefs. Mothers' employment does not necessarily have significant negative consequences for their children. In fact, for many mothers, working at paid jobs may enhance their relationship with their children. Moreover, evidence on day care from other modern societies—Czechoslovakia, East Germany, France, Greece, Hungary, Israel, and the Soviet Union—suggests that children are not harmed but rather are benefited in many ways.[29]

For instance, socialization researcher Urie Bronfenbrenner compared patterns of child rearing in the United States with those in the Soviet Union, where day care from infancy on is available. The conclusion was that Soviet children were more effectively socialized—that is, more effectively influenced, despite the fact that we as Christians would disagree with the content of that socialization. Bronfenbrenner's research also showed that Soviet children experience more companionship with their parents than American children.[30]

Admittedly, the evidence concerning the effects of day care on children, especially infants, is general in character and sparse in the context of American society. Yet for at least two reasons Christians ought seriously to consider joining the movement to establish good day-care centers of some type. First, many mothers simply have to work. Despite popular myths, the majority of working mothers are employed out of economic necessity.[31] Forty-three percent of working mothers with children under six have husbands whose income is insufficient to provide their families with what the government defines as the basic necessities of life. Besides these, many other working mothers with children under six work because they have been widowed, divorced, or deserted by their husbands and are now the family's chief economic provider. Certainly the children of these working women ought to be ensured good day care.

Second, task flexibility in marriage and the stewardship of talents by Christian marital partners would be enhanced by the availability of good day care. Its presence would give wives and husbands more options in deciding how they are going to accomplish family tasks. The decision to use or not to use such services would depend upon a responsible assessment of the needs of the child relative to the needs and talents of the parents.

Equal Rights For Women and Men. One of the most controversial pieces of legislation in the seventies has been the proposed twenty-third amendment to the U.S. Constitution—the Equal Rights Amendment (ERA). At first glance, the proposed amendment seems innocuous enough:

1. Equality of rights under the law shall not be denied or abridged by the United States or by any State on account of sex.
2. The Congress shall have the power to enforce, by appropriate legislation, the provisions of this article.
3. This amendment shall take effect two years after the date of ratification.

This amendment finally passed Congress in March, 1972 (it had been before each Congress since 1923) and was sent to the states for ratification. Three-fourths of the states—that is, thirty-eight—must ratify a proposed amendment within seven years in order for it to become law.

For a while, it looked as though the ERA would quickly win ratification. It had the support of the American Bar Association and of an impressive list of labor unions, women's groups, professional organizations, and religious organizations. But then there appeared antifeminist and anti-ERA groups like the Anti-Women's Liberation League, Happiness of Womanhood (HOW), Fascinating Womanhood, the Pussycat League, Women Who Want to be Women (WWWW), and STOP-ERA. These groups began to speak out against the ERA. Although many of their claims seemed extreme, many state legislators listened; and the process of ratification was slowed.

Whatever the outcome of this proposed law and its controversial effects, Christians ought to give serious consideration to the *main concept* behind the Equal Rights Amendment. How acceptable is the idea of equal standing for women and men before the law? A helpful way to approach the question is to review the controversy surrounding the ERA during the seventies.

The purpose of ERA is to "provide constitutional protection against laws and official practices that treat men and women differently."[32] According to the Citizens' Advisory Council on the Status of Women, at the time of congressional passage of the ERA there were still, for example, these forms of inequality:

1. State laws placing special restrictions on women with respect to hours of work and weightlifting on the job;
2. State laws prohibiting women from working in certain occupations;
3. Laws or practices operating to exclude women from State colleges and universities (including higher standards required for women applicants to institutions of higher learning and in the administration of scholarship programs);
4. Discrimination in employment by State and local governments;

5. Dual pay schedules for men and women public school teachers;
6. State laws providing for alimony to be awarded, under certain circumstances, to ex-wives but not to ex-husbands;
7. State laws placing special restrictions on the legal capacity of married women or on their right to establish a legal domicile;
8. State laws that require married women but not married men to go through a formal procedure and obtain court approval before they may engage in an independent business;
9. Social Security and other social benefits legislation which gives greater benefits to one sex than to the other;
10. Discriminatory preferences, based on sex, in child custody cases;
11. State laws providing that the *father* is the natural guardian of the minor children;
12. Different ages for males and females in (a) child labor laws, (b) age for marriage, (c) cutoff of the right to parental support, and (d) juvenile court jurisdiction;
13. Exclusion of women from the requirements of the Military Selective Service Act of 1967;
14. Special sex-based exemptions for women in selection of State jurors;
15. Heavier criminal penalties for female offenders than for male offenders committing the same crime.[33]

Although some of these laws had been struck down as unconstitutional under the equal-protection clause of the Fourteenth Amendment, most have remained in effect throughout the seventies.

Those who opposed the ERA, including many evangelical Christians, have directed their criticisms primarily at five areas. The first has to do with traditionally accepted practices of propriety between the sexes. Some critics have argued that under an ERA separate restrooms for men and women in public facilities and separate sleeping arrangements in prisons, military bases, and college dormitories would be unconstitutional. Those responding to these critics, however, point out that laws and their interpretation are very much grounded in a society's norms and values. It is improbable that the courts, in interpreting an equal-rights law, would ignore accepted community standards. Besides, the constitutional principle of the right to privacy, which has already been invoked by the courts in other connections, would be sufficient to ensure the separation of the sexes in any public facility for attending to personal bodily functions, sleeping, or disrobing.

A second area of criticism concerns compulsory military duty for women. A writer in one religious periodical asks: "How would you like your daughter to fight in combat and have an equal chance to become a POW?" [34] It is true that if conscription were reinstated, women would be equally subject to military duty under an ERA; but proponents argue that

> the requirement of service will be as unattractive and painful for them as it is now for many men.
>
> No one would suggest that combat service is pleasant or that the women who serve can avoid the possibility of physical harm and assault. But it is important to remember that all combat is dangerous, degrading and dehumanizing. This is true for all participants. As between brutalizing our young men and brutalizing our young women, there is little to choose. [35]

The point, advocates maintain, is that if women are ever to have full equality of opportunity with men before the law, they must also share fully in the responsibilities that it entails. This would extend to compulsory military service if that were reinstated.

Supporters of ERA contend that there are important additional dimensions to this matter of women in the military. First, in 1971, the year of the seventies during which the draft was calling up the most young men, only 1 percent of all men eligible to be taken were assigned to combat units, and only some of these actually saw action. [36] More importantly, the types of units to which women would be assigned under an ERA would depend on their individual characteristics. To be assigned to combat units, women would have to meet the same physical-fitness standards for such service as men. And finally, exemptions for care of children or other dependents, hardship, and physical disabilities would apply to women and men equally.

Historically, the participation of women in military services has been severely limited; as late as the early seventies the Women's Army Corps was permitted by law to constitute no more than 2 percent of the armed services. Under an ERA, such discrimination would have to end. Women would have "equal opportunity to enlist in the armed forces, and to receive valuable job training, educational benefits, medical benefits, retirement benefits, and all employment preferences accorded veterans."[37] As women continue to move into the competitive job market in greater numbers and to share the provider role in American society, equality of opportunity for such benefits affects that many more women than it did in the past.

The third area of concern relates to the effect of an ERA on certain laws involving sexual abuse. States one anti-ERA writer:

> With one stroke of the amending pen, 200 years of constitutional precedent designed to protect women will be wiped out. Laws against certain forms of sexual assault, statutory rape laws, consensual sodomy and adultery laws, and laws to protect women from enforced prostitution will vanish in a moment.[38]

ERA defenders claim this position reflects ignorance of a principle recognized by many legal scholars. Laws that deal with a physical characteristic unique to one sex would still be allowed under an ERA, since no matter how such laws are rewritten in sex-neutral terms, they would still apply only to one sex or the other.[39] Traditional rape laws are frequently cited as an example here. As for some other laws governing sexual conduct, an ERA would require that they be extended to cover not only the sex historically covered but the other sex as well. For instance, laws that traditionally have prohibited female prostitution would have to be extended to cover male prostitution as well.

Some critics have gone so far as to suggest that their individual right to establish the kind of family they wish to have would be destroyed. They maintain that an ERA would legislate full equality between spouses in family decision making, equal contributions by husband and wife to the economic support of the family, and no more alimony or child-support payments by former husbands in the case of divorce.[40] Advocates assert that an ERA would apply to areas of governmental action, not to the private relationships of men and women in the home. It would not outlaw patriarchal family structures—or, for that matter, matriarchal ones. In the matter of supporting the family, an ERA would demand only that any laws about economic providing in the family would be written in a sex-neutral fashion. This means that both spouses could work if they wished to, or that if one spouse were the primary wage earner while the other stayed home to tend things there, the first spouse would be required to provide economic support for the second. Finally, argue supporters, alimony and child-support responsibilities would not disappear under an ERA. Rather, laws governing them would be shaped without regard to sex. Hence child support after a divorce would be determined on the basis of each spouse's independent resources, earning power, and the like. The same principle would be applied to the custody of children after a divorce. Judges would be required to examine the needs of children relative to the individual characteristics of the former spouses, instead of taking only gender into account.

A final set of criticisms has come from certain members of the legal community.[41] Among the more common is the claim that an ERA is superfluous since it would guarantee little more than what is already granted under the equal-protection clause of the Fourteenth Amendment. Second, there is the argument that under an ERA the courts would be jammed with litigation testing its precise implications. In answer to the first claim Kathleen Willert Peratis and Susan Deller Ross, lawyers for the American Civil Liberties Union, argue:

> The equal-protection clause of the 14th Amendment was adopted after the Civil War for one central purpose—to prohibit race discrimination. Not until 1971 did the Supreme Court rule in favor of women who complained of unconstitutional sex discrimination. Since then, the Court has upheld sex discrimination in some cases and rejected it in others.
>
> The ERA would provide the equal protection principle in all cases of sex discrimination.[42]

Moreover, state Peratis and Ross, the most likely alternative to reform by a constitutional amendment would be statutory reform. But they see this as a piecemeal principle of equality before the law regardless of sex.[43] As to the argument that an ERA would inevitably lead to excessive litigation, defenders point to New Mexico and Pennsylvania, which incorporated an equal-rights provision into their state law. In New Mexico, where the legislature quickly altered its laws to conform to its new legal principle, little litigation has resulted from the equal-rights law. Pennsylvania, which did not quickly change its discriminatory laws, experienced much needed litigation directed toward bringing existing laws into line with its equal-rights law.[44]

Clearly, the ERA of the seventies has been a hotly debated proposal. Evangelical Christians themselves are divided on the issue. As of this writing, it appears that the ratification of the ERA of the seventies is uncertain, although the time for individual state approval has been extended. However, since an ERA has been under consideration in some manner ever since 1923, the proposal, if defeated, will likely soon be revived. We believe that

Christians ought to give serious consideration to the *basic principle* behind an equal-rights law—that of neither denying nor conferring rights differentially by sex. In our opinion, this concept is sound and ought to be supported, whatever the outcome of the present ERA or a future one.

Historically, certain laws or the manner in which they have been interpreted have served to reinforce traditional sex roles. An example is the law by which mothers (but not fathers) with children under a specified age are exempt from jury duty. Another is the common court practice of giving the mother custody of the children after a divorce almost regardless of the individual circumstances involved. Clearly these laws are saying something about the expected roles for women and men.

If task flexibility and stewardship of talents are ever to be more fully practiced, certainly one of the first requirements is that society have a system of justice under which judgments are made on the basis of the actual capabilities and functions of people, not according to artificially limiting sex-role stereotypes.

Conclusion

In every known human society, men have held the most highly valued positions, have been thought to have the most valuable personal attributes, and have dominated women. We as Christians can recognize these facts as an expression of the curse in Genesis 3, but at the same time we must attempt to live out the redemptive vision of the gospel for the male-female relationship. Social conditions today offer a greater opportunity than ever before for flexibility in the social roles of women and men. This should give us cause to rejoice. Rather than living by restrictive sex-role stereotypes, we now have a greater chance to allocate responsibilities on the basis of God-given talents and to develop personal identities based on the fruit of the Spirit. If we respond to this opportunity, we may expect the invidious social distinctions between the sexes and the tensions that flow from those distinctions to recede. At the same time, we may derive comfort from knowing that when Christian spouses try to exercise stewardship of gifts in meeting their family responsibilities, they are more closely approximating the relationship for men and women in marriage intended by God—an organic unity of complementary partners.

Discussion Questions

1/ Why do employed wives have more influence in family decisions than nonemployed wives?

2/ Assume you are married, both you and your spouse are employed full-time, and you have a baby. Do you think you should withdraw from the labor force? Do you think your spouse should? Why or why not?

3/ In this chapter we looked at data on the consequences of married women's employment for their children, their husbands, and themselves. Has this altered your opinion about the advisability of this practice among Christians? If so, in what way?

4/ Does your church do anything to help dual-career families (families in which both spouses are employed) with their particular problems? If so, what? If not, why do you think it does not? Do you think it should?

5/ Do you agree with the basic principle behind the ERA? Why or why not?

6/ Do you think Christians ought to support the movement for more day-care centers? Why or why not?

7/ Besides the social changes discussed in this and the previous chapter, what others might further the two principles advocated, stewardship of individual talents and identities based on the fruit of the Spirit regardless of sex?

8/ How is the Christian perspective on sex roles presented in this book different from that espoused by the moderate element of the feminist movement?

Suggested Readings

Carlson, G. William. "**ERA: Fairness or Fraud?**" *Eternity* 26 (November 1975), pp. 28-31, 68-75.

Carlson, a Christian professor of political science, sets down certain arguments as to why he believes evangelical Christians ought to be sympathetic to the principle of equal rights for women and men before the law. Juxtaposed to

Carlson's article is one in which Margaret N. Bornhouse highlights the "protective legislation" for women that would be lost under an ERA. In combination, the articles give a useful summary of what is at stake for Christians in the ERA controversy.

Curtis, Jean. **Working Mothers.** Garden City, New York: Doubleday & Co., 1976.

Using interview data, Curtis details the sorts of problems faced by dual-career families. The larger share of this helpful book is given to describing the ways in which these families have come to cope with their difficulties.

Hoffman, Lois Wladis, and F. Ivan Nye. **Working Mothers: An Evaluative Review of the Consequences for Wife, Husband, and Child.** San Francisco: Jossey-Bass Publishers, 1974.

A compendium of research findings about the results of working mothers' employment for members of the family. Dispels many current cultural beliefs.

Roby, Pamela, ed. **Child Care—Who Cares?** New York: Basic Books, 1973.

An informative anthology that traces the history of child care in the United States, shows the acute need for additional child-care programs, and suggests some innovative programs based in part upon an evaluation of programs in other countries.

NOTES
/1/

1/ These descriptions of traditional male and female roles are consistent with sociological analyses of those roles. See, for example, Clifford Kirkpatrick, **The Family as Process and Institution** (New York: The Ronald Press Co., 1963), p. 168; and Ruth Shonle Cavan, **The American Family** (New York: Thomas Y. Crowell Co., 1969), p. 34.

2/ U.S. Bureau of the Census, **Historical Statistics of the United States: Colonial Times to 1957** (Washington, D.C.: U.S. Government Printing Office, 1960), pp. 57-71.

3/ William F. Ogburn and Clark Tibbitts, "The Family and Its Functions," Report of the President's Research Committee on Social Trends, **Recent Social Trends in the United States** (New York: McGraw-Hill Book Co., 1934), pp. 661-708.

4/ Arnold M. Rose, "The Adequacy of Women's Expectations for Adult Roles," **Social Forces** 30 (October 1951), p. 70.

5/ Gerald R. Leslie, **The Family in Social Context** (New York: Oxford University Press, 1967), pp. 234-35.

6/ Leslie Aldridge Westoff and Charles F. Westoff, **From Now to Zero: Fertility, Contraception and Abortion in America** (Boston: Little, Brown & Co., 1971), p. 45.

7/ See Ruth B. Dixon, "Hallelujah the Pill?," **Transaction** 8 (November-December 1970), p. 44.

8/ William Peterson, **Population** (New York: Macmillan Publishing Co., 1975), p. 533.

9/ Evelyn Millis Duvall, **Family Development** (Philadelphia: J. B. Lippincott Co., 1971), pp. 107-9.

10/ Talcott Parsons, "Age and Sex in the Social Structure of the United States," **American Sociological Review** 7 (October 1942), pp. 611-12.

11/ In fact, this increase may be apparent rather than real, since the U.S. Bureau of the Census changed its techniques and its definition of labor status during the same period. A discussion of these changes and their effects on the rates of female labor-force participation appears in Robert W. Smuts, "The Female Labor Force," **Journal of the American Statistical Association,** March 1960, pp. 71-79.

12/ Stephen J. Bahr, "Effects on Power and Division of Labor in the Family," in **Working Mothers,** ed. Lois Wladis Hoffman and F. Ivan Nye (San Francisco: Jossey-Bass Publishers, 1974), pp. 184-85.

13/ Ibid.

14/ See Deborah Babcox and Madeline Belkin, eds., **Liberation Now** (New York: Dell Publishing Co., 1971), p. 3.

15/ See Jo Freeman, "The Women's Liberation Movement: Its Origins, Structure, Impact, and Ideas," in **Women: A Feminist Perspective,** ed. Jo Freeman (Palo Alto, Calif.: Mayfield Publishing Co., 1975), p. 457.

16/ F. Ivan Nye and Felix M. Berardo, **The Family: Its Structure and Interaction** (New York: The Macmillan Co., 1973), pp. 278-79.

17/ Francine D. Blau, "Women in the Labor Force: An Overview," in Freeman, **Women,** p. 221.

18/ Ibid., pp. 222-24.

19/ For an analysis of the composition of the women's movement, see Barbara Bovee Polk, "Women's Liberation: Movement for Equality," in **Toward a Sociology of Women,** ed. Constantina Safilios-Rothschild (Lexington, Mass.: Xerox College Publishing, 1972), pp. 321-30. Much of the following discussion relies on this source.

20/ Freeman, "Women's Liberation Movement," p. 450.

21/ For a list of the accomplishments of women's rights groups, see ibid., p. 453.

22/ G. C. Berkouwer, "Understanding Scripture," **Christianity Today** 14 (22 May 1970), p. 40.

23/ Letha Scanzoni and Nancy Hardesty, **All We're Meant to Be** (Waco, Texas: Word Books, 1974), p. 18.

24/ For example, the functional theory of social inequality maintains that the only way to motivate people to play different occupational roles in society is to have a system of differing individual rewards. The implication is that people are basically self-interested, a characteristic that Christians know resulted from the Fall. See Kingsley Davis and Wilbert E. Moore, "Some Principles of Stratification," **American Sociological Review** 10 (April 1945), pp. 242-49.

25/ An excellent consideration of how the individual influences and is influenced by social interaction is contained in Peter L. Berger, **Invitation to Sociology: A Humanistic Perspective** (New York: Doubleday & Co., 1963).

26/ For a complete discussion of this definition see Alan P. Bates, **The Sociological Enterprise** (Boston: Houghton Mifflin Co., 1967), pp. 4-29.

27/ An informative consideration of why Christian evangelicals have shied away from evaluating societal structures and from engaging in social activism based on this evaluation is contained in Paul B. Henry, **Politics for Evangelicals** (Valley Forge: Judson Press, 1974), pp. 27-58.

/2/

1/ See John Money and Anke A. Ehrhardt, **Man and Woman, Boy and Girl: The Differentiation and Dimorphism of Gender Identity From Conception to Maturity** (Baltimore: The Johns Hopkins University Press, 1972), and John Money and Patricia Tucker, **Sexual Signatures: On Being a Man or a Woman** (Boston: Little, Brown & Co., 1975). The second book is largely a less technical adaptation of the first.

2/ Money's description of these forks can be found in Money and Tucker, **Sexual Signatures,** pp. 41-49.

3/ Clarice Stasz Stoll, **Female and Male: Socialization, Social Roles and Social Structure** (Dubuque, Iowa: William C. Brown Co., Publishers, 1974), p. 2.

4/ For diagrams of this and later stages of embryonic development see Money and Ehrhardt, **Man and Woman,** p. 41; or Money and Tucker, **Sexual Signatures,** p. 45.

5/ Money and Tucker, **Sexual Signatures,** p. 47.

6/ For a full description of this and other hermaphroditic conditions see Money and Ehrhardt, **Man and Woman.**

7/ Edmund W. Overstreet, "The Biological Make-up of Women," in **The Potential of Women,** ed. Seymour M. Farber and Roger H. L. Wilson (New York: McGraw-Hill Book Co., 1963), pp. 21-22.

8/ Mary E. Moore, "Physical Changes," in **Aging and Society,** ed. Matilda White Riley (New York: Russell Sage Foundation, 1968).

9/ Ann Crittenden Scott, "Closing the Muscle Gap," **Ms.,** September 1974, p. 55.

10/ Ibid., p. 49.

11/ See A. H. Norris, T. Lundy, and N. W. Shock, "Trends in Selected Indices of Body Composition in Men Between the Ages 30 and 80 Years," **Annals of the New York Academy of Sciences** 110 (1963), p. 623; and C. Young, "Body Composition of Young Women," **Journal of the American Dietary Association** 38 (1961), pp. 332-40.

12/ For a discussion of this and other differences of physique that play a role in the strength differential between the sexes see Ellen W. Gerber et al., **The American Woman in Sport** (Reading, Mass.: Addison-Wesley Publishing Co., 1974), pp. 446-53.

13/ Ibid., pp. 475-84.

14/ Money and Tucker, **Sexual Signatures,** p. 42.

15/ Ashley Montagu, **The Natural Superiority of Women** (New York: Macmillan Publishing Co., 1974), p. 85.

16/ Ibid., p. 80.

17/ For a full listing of these sex-linked disorders, see ibid., pp. 82-84.

18/ For more about sex differences in susceptibility to disease, see David A. Hamburg and Donald T. Lunde, "Sex Hormones in the Development of Sex Differences in Human Behavior," in **The Development of Sex Differences,** ed. Eleanor E. Maccoby (Stanford: Stanford University Press, 1966), pp. 19-20; and Montagu, **Natural Superiority,** pp. 87-89.

19/ Francis C. Madigan, "Are Sex Mortality Differentials Biologically Caused?," **The Milbank Memorial Fund Quarterly** 35 (April 1957), pp. 202-23.

20/ For an entire book devoted to this thesis, see Steven Goldberg, **The Inevitability of Patriarchy** (New York: William Morrow & Co., 1973).

21/ Klaus R. Scherer, Ronald P. Abeles, and Claude S. Fischer, **Human Aggression and Conflict** (Englewood Cliffs, N.J.: Prentice-Hall, 1975), pp. 2-5.

22/ For the most complete available summary of research on aggression and the sexes, see Eleanor Emmons Maccoby and Carol Nagy Jacklin, **The Psychology of Sex Differences** (Stanford: Stanford University Press, 1974), pp. 227-42.

23/ Beatrice Whiting and Carolyn Pope, "A Cross-Cultural Analysis of Sex Differences in the Behavior of Children Aged Three to Eleven," **Journal of Social Psychology** 91 (December 1973), pp. 171-88.

24/ Maccoby and Jacklin, **Psychology,** pp. 229-47.

25/ For summaries of this evidence, see ibid., pp. 243-47; Money and Ehrhardt, **Man and Woman,** pp. 95-114; and Money and Tucker, **Sexual Signatures,** pp. 63-82.

26/ Judith M. Bardwick, **Psychology of Women: A Study of Bio-Cultural Conflicts** (New York: Harper & Row Publishers, 1971), pp. 24-25.

27/ For a summary of the findings of the researchers, see ibid., pp. 26-33.

28/ Ibid., p. 32.

29/ Katherina Dalton, **The Premenstrual Syndrome** (Springfield, Ill.: C. C. Thomas, 1964).

30/ Bardwick, **Women,** pp. 37-38.

31/ Maccoby and Jacklin, **Psychology,** pp. 169-90.

32/ For a review of the research on estrogen therapy, see Bardwick, **Women,** pp. 35-39.

33/ Maccoby and Jacklin, **Psychology,** pp. 214-15.

34/ Lionel Tiger, "Male Dominance? Yes, Alas, A Sexist Plot: No." in John A. Perry and Murray B. Seidler, **Contemporary Society** (San Francisco: Canfield Press, 1972), p. 41.

35/ Jay S. Rosenblatt, "The Development of Maternal Responsiveness in the Rat," **American Journal of Orthropsychiatry** 39 (1969), pp. 36-56.

36/ Money and Tucker, **Sexual Signatures,** pp. 74-75.

37/ Money and Ehrhardt, **Man and Woman,** p. 101.

38/ See Gary Mitchell, William K. Redican, and Jody Gomber, "Males Can Raise Babies," **Psychology Today,** April 1974, pp. 63-68.

39/ Ruth Shonle Cavan, **The American Family** (New York: Thomas Y. Crowell Co., 1969), p. 378.

40/ Money and Ehrhardt, **Man and Woman,** pp. 217-22.

41/ Herant A. Katchadourian and Donald T. Lunde, **Fundamentals of Human Sexuality** (New York: Holt, Rinehart & Winston, 1975), p. 93.

42/ Money and Ehrhardt, **Man and Woman,** pp. 220-21.

43/ Ibid., p. 219.

44/ Ibid.

45/ Clellan S. Ford and Frank A. Beach, **Patterns of Sexual Behavior** (New York: Harper & Row Publishers, 1951), p. 110.

46/ Ibid., p. 267.

47/ Money and Tucker, **Sexual Signatures,** p. 38.

/3/

1/ For a detailed sociological discussion of status and role see Robert Bierstedt, **The Social Order** (New York: McGraw-Hill Book Co., 1974), pp. 250-79.

2/ George P. Murdock, "Comparative Data on the Division of Labor by Sex," **Social Forces** 15 (May 1937), pp. 551-53.

3/ George P. Murdock, **Social Structure** (New York: The Macmillan Co., 1949), pp. 7-8. See also Bierstedt, **Social Order,** pp. 392-94.

4/ William A. Haviland, **Cultural Anthropology** (New York: Holt, Rinehart & Winston, 1975), p. 139.

5/ William Peterson, **Population** (New York: Macmillan Publishing Co., 1975), p. 378.

6/ Although the bulk of the evidence strongly suggests that males hold the dominant positions in all human societies, it should be noted that this long-accepted conclusion has been challenged; see Susan Carol Rogers, "Female Forms of Power and the Myth of Male Dominance: A Model of Female/Male Interaction in Peasant Society," **American Ethnologist** 2 (November 1975), pp. 727-56.

7/ Murdock, **Social Structure,** p. 7.

8/ Peterson, **Population,** p. 272.

9/ Judith K. Brown, "A Note on the Division of Labor by Sex," **American Anthropologist** 72 (October 1970), p. 1073. Also see George P. Murdock and Caterina Provost, "Factors in the Division of Labor by Sex: A Cross-Cultural Analysis," **Ethnology** 12 (April 1973), pp. 203-25.

10/ Joel Aronoff and William D. Crano, "A Re-examination of the Cross-Cultural Principles of Task Segregation and Sex-Role Differentiation in the Family," **American Sociological Review** 40 (February 1975), pp. 12-20. For the original data source see George P. Murdock, "Ethnographic Atlas: A Summary," **Ethnology** 6 (April 1967), pp. 109-236.

11/ Jean D. Grambs and Walter B. Waetjen, **Sex: Does It Make a Difference?** (Belmont, Calif.: Wadsworth Publishing Co., 1975), pp. 13-16.

12/ Colin M. Turnbull, **The Forest People** (New York: Simon & Schuster, 1962), pp. 131-32.

13/ Margaret Mead, **Male and Female** (New York: William Morrow & Co., 1949).

14/ Steven Goldberg, **The Inevitability of Patriarchy** (New York: William Morrow & Co., 1974).

15/ Margaret Mead, **Sex and Temperament in Three Primitive Societies** (New York: Mentor Books, 1950), p. 6.

16/ Ashley Montagu, **The Natural Superiority of Women** (New York: Macmillan Publishing Co., 1974), p. 61.

/4/

1/ Lucile Duberman, **Gender and Sex in Society** (New York: Praeger Publishers, 1975), p. 23.

2/ Dushkin Publishing Group, **Encyclopedia of Sociology** (Guilford, Conn.: Dushkin Publishing Group, 1974), p. 272.

3/ Ibid.

4/ Susan Goldberg and Michael Lewis, "Play Behavior in the Year-Old Infant: Early Sex Differences," **Child Development** 40 (March-June 1969), pp. 21-31.

5/ Ibid., p. 29.

6/ Lenore J. Weitzman, "Sex-Role Socialization," in **Women: A Feminist Perspective,** ed. Jo Freeman (Palo Alto, Calif.: Mayfield Publishing Co., 1975), p. 109. This article is a comprehensive summary of the social-scientific research on sex-role socialization.

7/ Meyer Rabban, "Sex-Role Identification in Young Children in Two

Diverse Social Groups," **Genetic Psychology Monographs** 42 (1950), pp. 85-141.

8/ Mirra Komarovsky, **Women in the Modern World** (Boston: Little, Brown & Co., 1953), p. 55.

9/ Weitzman, "Sex-Role Socialization," p. 110.

10/ Lenore J. Weitzman et al., "Sex-Role Socialization in Picture Books for Preschool Children," **The American Journal of Sociology** 77 (May 1972), pp. 1125-50.

11/ Ibid., pp. 1139-46.

12/ Ibid., p. 1143.

13/ Jo Ann Gardner, "Sesame Street and Sex-Role Stereotypes," **Woman** 1 (Spring 1970), p. 42.

14/ Carole Joffe, "Sex Role Socialization and the Nursery School: As the Twig Is Bent," in **Sex: Male/Gender: Masculine**, ed. John W. Petras (Port Washington, New York: Alfred Publishing Co., 1975), pp. 104-19.

15/ For an examination of the relative merits of different learning theories as they apply to sex-role development in children, see Paul H. Mussen, "Early Sex-Role Development," in **Handbook of Socialization Theory and Research**, ed. David A. Goslin (Chicago: Rand McNally and Co., 1969), pp. 707-31.

16/ Jerome Kagan, "Acquisition and Significance of Sex Typing and Sex Role Identity," in Martin L. Hoffman and Lois W. Hoffman, **Review of Child Development Research: Volume One** (New York: Russell Sage Foundation, 1964), pp. 137-45. See also Daniel G. Brown, "Sex Role Preference in Young Children," **Psychological Monographs** 70 (1956), pp. 1-19; and Willard W. Hartup and Elsie A. Zook, "Sex Role Preferences in Three-and-Four-Year-Old Children," **Journal of Consulting Psychology** 24 (December 1960), pp. 420-26.

17/ Irvin L. Child, Elmer H. Potter, and Estelle H. Levine, "Children's Textbooks and Personality Development: An Exploration in the Social Psychology of Education," in **Human Development: Selected Readings,** ed. Morris L. Haimowitz and Natalie R. Haimowitz (New York: Thomas Y. Crowell Co., 1960), pp. 292-305.

18/ Ibid., p. 302.

19/ Laurel A. Marten and Margaret W. Matlin, "Does Sexism in Elementary Readers Still Exist?," **The Reading Teacher** 29 (May 1976), pp. 764-70. See also Dianne Bennet Graehner, "A Decade of Sexism in Readers," **The Reading Teacher** 26 (October 1972), pp. 52-58; and Anne Stevens Fishman, "A Criticism of Sexism in Elementary Readers," **The Reading Teacher** 29 (February 1976), pp. 443-46.

20/ Marten and Matlin, "Elementary Readers," p. 767.

21/ Terry N. Saario, Carol Nagy Jacklin, and Carol Kehr Tittle, "Sex-Role Stereotyping in the Public Schools," **Harvard Educational Review** 43 (August 1973), pp. 399-405.

22/ Ruth E. Hartley, "Sex-Role Pressures and the Socialization of the Male Child," **Psychological Reports** 5 (1959), pp. 457-68.

23/ Ibid., pp. 460-61.

24/ Ibid., pp. 461-62.

25/ Ibid., p. 461.

26/ Ibid., p. 462.

27/ Saario, Jacklin, and Tittle, "Sex-Role Stereotyping," pp. 405-7.

28/ Ibid., pp. 408-9.

29/ James S. Coleman, **The Adolescent Society** (New York: The Free Press of Glencoe, 1961).

30/ Ibid., p. 37.

31/ See, for example, Weitzman, "Sex-Role Socialization," p. 126.

32/ David R. Matteson, **Adolescence Today: Sex Roles and the Search for Identity** (Homewood, Ill.: The Dorsey Press, 1975), pp. 76-79.

33/ Weitzman, "Sex-Role Socialization," p. 126.

34/ David F. Aberle and Kaspar D. Naegele, "Middle-class Fathers' Occupational Role and Attitudes Toward Children," in **A Modern Introduction to the Family,** ed. Norman W. Bell and Ezra F. Vogel (New York: The Free Press of Glencoe, 1960), pp. 126-36.

35/ Ibid., p. 132.

36/ Ibid.

37/ William H. Sewell and Vimal P. Shah, "Social Class, Parental Encouragement, and Educational Aspirations," **The American Journal of Sociology** 73 (March 1968), pp. 559-72.

38/ Lovelle Ray, "The American Women in Mass Media: How Much Emancipation and What Does It Mean?" in **Toward a Sociology of Women,** ed. Constantina Safilios-Rothschild (Lexington, Mass.: Xerox College Publishing, 1972), pp. 41-62.

39/ Ibid., p. 59.

40/ Margaret B. Lefkowitz, "The Women's Magazine Short-Story Heroine in 1957 and 1967," in ibid., pp. 37-40.

41/ Ibid., p. 39.

42/ Harvey Cox, **The Secular City** (New York: The Macmillan Co., 1965), p. 58.

43/ Ibid., p. 59.

44/ Lucy Komisar, "The Image of Woman in Advertising," in **Women in Sexist Society: Studies in Power and Powerlessness,** ed. Vivian Gornick and Barbara Moran (New York: Basic Books, Publishers, 1971), p. 207-17.

45/ Ibid., pp. 208-10.

46/ Bernard Rosenberg and David Manning White, eds., **Mass Culture** (New York: The Free Press of Glencoe, 1957), p. 342.
47/ See National Report, "The Television Image of Women," **Intellect** 103 (April 1975).
48/ Ibid.,
49/ Kay F. Reinartz, "The Paper Doll: Images of American Woman in Popular Songs," in Safilios-Rothschild, **Sociology of Women,** pp. 293-308.
50/ Ibid., p. 306.
51/ Mirra Komarovsky, "Cultural Contradictions and Sex Roles," **American Journal of Sociology** 52 (November 1946), pp. 184-89.
52/ National Report, "Television Image."
53/ For an overview of these variations see Weitzman, "Sex-Role Socialization," pp. 118-20.
54/ Inge K. Broverman et al., "Sex-Role Stereotypes: A Current Appraisal," in **Women and Achievement: Social and Motivational Analyses,** ed. Martha Tamara Shuch Mednick, Sandra Schwartz Tangri, and Lois Wladis Hoffman (New York: John Wiley & Sons, 1975), pp. 32-47.

/5/

1/ For definitions and a more detailed discussion of achieved and ascribed roles see Ronald C. Federico, **Sociology** (Reading, Mass.: Addison-Wesley Publishing Co., 1975), pp. 121-29.
2/ Francine D. Blau, "Women in the Labor Force: An Overview," in **Women: A Feminist Perspective,** ed. Jo Freeman (Palo Alto, Calif.: Mayfield Publishing Co., 1975), pp. 221.
3/ Valerie Kincade Oppenheimer, "The Sex-Labelling of Jobs," in **Women and Achievement: Social and Motivational Analyses,** ed. Martha Tamara Shuch Mednick, Sandra Schwartz Tangri, and Lois Wladis Hoffman (New York: John Wiley & Sons, 1975), pp. 307-25.
4/ Edward Gross, "Plus Ca Change. . .? The Sexual Structure of Occupations Over Time," **Social Problems** 16 (Fall 1968), pp. 198-208.
5/ Ibid., p. 202.
6/ U.S. Department of Labor, Employment Standards Administration, Women's Bureau, "The Earnings Gap Between Women and Men," 1976, p. 6.
7/ Teresa Levitin, Robert P. Quinn, and Graham L. Staines, "Sex Dis-

crimination Against the American Working Woman," in Mednick, Tangri, and Hoffman, **Women and Achievement,** pp. 326-38.

8/ Gail Falk, "Sex Discrimination in the Trade Unions: Legal Resources for Change," in Freeman, **Women,** p. 273.

9/ Ibid., p. 268.

10/ Jo Freeman, **The Politics of Women's Liberation: A Case Study of an Emerging Social Movement and Its Relation to the Policy Process** (New York: David McKay Co., 1975), pp. 188-90.

11/ Thomas F. Pettigrew, **Racially Separate or Together** (New York: McGraw-Hill Book Co., 1971), pp. 64-69.

12/ Philip Goldberg, "Are Women Prejudiced Against Women?" **Transaction,** April 1968, pp. 28-30.

13/ Ibid., p. 30.

14/ Ibid.

15/ Matina S. Horner, "Toward an Understanding of Achievement-Related Conflicts in Women," **Journal of Social Issues** 28 (1972), pp. 157-75.

16/ Ibid., pp. 162-63.

17/ See, for example, Deborah S. David and Robert Brannon, eds., **The Forty-nine Percent Majority: The Male Sex Role** (Reading, Mass.: Addison-Wesley Publishing Co., 1976); or Joseph H. Pleck and Jack Sawyer, eds., **Men and Masculinity** (Englewood Cliffs, N.J.: Prentice-Hall, 1974).

/6/

1/ Nahum M. Sarna, **Understanding Genesis** (New York: McGraw-Hill Book Co., 1966).

2/ Paul K. Jewett, **Man as Male and Female** (Grand Rapids: William B. Eerdmans Publishing Co., 1975); Karl Barth, **Church Dogmatics** (Edinburgh, Scotland: T & T Clark, 1961).

3/ Harold G. Stigers, **A Commentary on Genesis** (Grand Rapids: Zondervan Publishing House, 1976).

4/ Clarence J. Vos, **Women in Old Testament Worship** (Delft, The Netherlands: N.V. Verenigde Drukkerijen Judels & Brinkman, 1968).

5/ For an extended discussion of John Calvin's view of women see Willis P. De Boer, "Calvin on the Role of Women," in **Exploring the Heritage of John Calvin,** ed. David E. Holwerda (Grand Rapids: Baker Book House, 1976), pp. 236-72.

6/ Vos, **Women,** p. 18.

7/ See James Plastaras, **Creation and Covenant** (Milwaukee: The Bruce Publishing Co., 1968), pp. 39-40.

8/ See, for example, H. C. Leupold, **Exposition of Genesis,** Vol. 1 (Grand Rapids: Baker Book House, 1956), p. 172; and Stigers, **Commentary,** p. 80.

9/ Vos, **Women,** pp. 24-25.

10/ E. A. Speiser, **The Anchor Bible: Genesis** (New York: Doubleday & Co., 1964).

11/ C. F. Keil and F. Delitzsch, **Biblical Commentary on the Old Testament: The Pentateuch,** Vol. 1, trans. James Martin (Grand Rapids: William B. Eerdmans Publishing Co., n.d.), p. 103.

12/ For treatments of the concept *head* see: H. L. E. Luering, "Head," in **The International Standard Bible Encyclopedia** (Grand Rapids: William B. Eerdmans Publishing Co., 1955), pp. 1348-49; Heinrich Schlier, "Kephale," in **Theological Dictionary of the New Testament,** Vol. 3, ed. Gerhard Kittel, trans. Geoffrey W. Bromiley (Grand Rapids: William B. Eerdmans Publishing Co., 1965), p. 673-82; and Colin Brown, "Head," in **The New International Dictionary of New Testament Theology,** Vol. 2 (Exeter, Devon, U.K.: The Paternoster Press; Grand Rapids: Zondervan Publishing House), pp. 156-63.

13/ Ibid., p. 159.

14/ See Jewett, **Man,** pp. 66-68, and De Boer, "Calvin."

15/ See Letha Scanzoni and Nancy Hardesty, **All We're Meant to Be** (Waco, Texas: Word Books, 1974).

16/ See John Vriend, "Man & Woman: Co-ordinates in Christ," **The Banner** 110 (11 April 1975), pp. 10-11.

17/ Krister Stendahl, **The Bible and the Role of Women** (Philadelphia: Fortress Press, 1966), p. 37.

18/ Ibid., p. 35.

19/ Ibid., p. 37.

20/ Kittel, **Dictionary,** Vol. 1, p. 777.

21/ Ibid., pp. 781-84. See also Stendahl, **Role of Women,** pp. 25-28.

22/ Jewett, **Man,** p. 94.

23/ For more on this point see Scanzoni and Hardesty, **Meant to Be,** pp. 67-69.

24/ As quoted in Gloria Steinem, "The Myth of Masculine Mystique," **International Education** 1 (1972), p. 32.

25/ Robert Ringer, **Winning Through Intimidation** (Greenwich, Conn.: Fawcett Publications, 1976), pp. 40-43, 123-32.

26/ Simone de Beauvoir and Betty Friedan, "Sex, Society, and the Female Dilemma: A Dialogue," **Saturday Review,** 14 June 1975, pp. 12-20.

/7/

1/ Mary Bouma, "Liberated Mothers," **Christianity Today** 15 (7 May 1971), p. 5.

2/ Ibid., p. 6.

3/ Very complete summaries of the many studies relating to the effects of married women's employment on family members are contained in Lois Wladis Hoffman and F. Ivan Nye, eds., **Working Mothers: An Evaluative Review of the Consequences for Wife, Husband, and Child** (San Francisco: Jossey-Bass Publishers, 1974); and F. Ivan Nye and Felix M. Berardo, **The Family: Its Structure and Interaction** (New York: The Macmillan Co., 1973), pp. 269-313. Much of the content of this section is based on those works.

4/ See, for instance, John Bowlby, **Child Care and the Growth of Love** (Geneva, Switzerland: World Health Organization, 1952).

5/ Nye and Berardo, **Family**, p. 282.

6/ See Lois Wladis Hoffman, "Effects on Child," in Hoffman and Nye, **Working Mothers**, pp. 137-39.

7/ Ibid., pp. 140-42.

8/ Ibid., p. 142.

9/ Nye and Berardo, **Family**, pp. 282-83.

10/ Ibid., pp. 283-84.

11/ Ibid., p. 284.

12/ For a summary of this research, see Hoffman, "Effects on Child," pp. 129-33.

13/ Inge Broverman et al., "Sex-Role Stereotypes: A Current Appraisal," in **Women and Achievement: Social and Motivational Analyses,** ed. Martha Tamara Shuch Mednick, Sandra Schwartz Tangri, and Lois Wladis Hoffman (New York: John Wiley & Sons, 1975), pp. 43-44.

14/ See Stephen J. Bahr, "Effects on Power and Division of Labor in the Family," in Hoffman and Nye, **Working Mothers**, pp. 167-81.

15/ David M. Heer, "Dominance and the Working Wife," in **The Employed Mother in America,** ed. F. Ivan Nye and Lois Wladis Hoffman, (Chicago: Rand McNally & Co., 1963), pp. 251-62.

16/ Nye and Berardo, **Family**, p. 286.

17/ Ibid., pp. 286-88.

18/ Ibid., p. 288.

19/ Ibid.

20/ F. Ivan Nye, "Effects on Mother," in Hoffman and Nye, **Working Mothers,** pp. 208-9.

21/ Ibid., pp. 212-13.

22/ Ibid., pp. 211-12.
23/ See Nye and Berardo, **Family,** p. 290.
24/ For an empirically based, detailed look at the ways in which working women and their families cope with their circumstances, see Jean Curtis, **Working Mothers** (Garden City, N.Y.: Doubleday & Co., 1976).
25/ Rosalyn F. Baxandall, "Who Shall Care for Our Children? The History and Development of Day Care in the United States," in **Women: A Feminist Perspective,** ed. Jo Freeman (Palo Alto, Calif.: Mayfield Publishing Co., 1975), pp. 89-93.
26/ Ibid., p. 93.
27/ See Pamela Roby, "Child Care—What and Why?," in **Child Care—Who Cares?,** ed. Pamela Roby (New York: Basic Books, 1973), pp. 4-5.
28/ See Baxandall, Who Shall Care?," pp. 93-94.
29/ See Dale Meers and Allen Mararns, "Group Care of Infants in Other Countries," in **Early Child Care: The New Perspectives,** ed. Laura L. Dittman (New York: Atherton, 1968), pp. 234-82.
30/ See Urie Bronfenbrenner, **Two Worlds of Childhood: U.S. and U.S.S.R.** (New York: Russell Sage Foundation, 1970).
31/ Roby, "Child Care," p. 3.
32/ Citizens' Advisory Council on the Status of Women, "The Proposed Equal Rights Amendment to the United States Constitution" (Washington, D.C.: U.S. Government Printing Office, 1970), p. 1.
33/ Ibid., pp. 3-4.
34/ Pat Brooks, editorial on ERA, **Christian Life** 37 (July 1975), p. 25.
35/ As quoted in "'I Didn't Raise My Girl to Be a Soldier': Sense and Nonsense About the ERA," **The Christian Century** 89 (25 October 1972), p. 1058.
36/ G. William Carlson, "ERA: Fairness or Fraud?," **Eternity** 26 (November 1975), p. 71.
37/ Kathleen Willert Peratis and Susan Deller Ross, "A Primer on the ERA," **Ms.** 5 (January 1977), p. 76. The authors are lawyers on the national staff of the American Civil Liberties Union and serve as counsel for that organization.
38/ Brooks, Editorial, p. 25.
39/ Citizens' Advisory Council on the Status of Women, "Proposed Amendment," p. 13.
40/ Brooks, editorial, pp. 25-26.
41/ See, for example, Charles M. Whelan, "ERA: A Lawyer's Doubts," **America** 132 (17 May 1975), pp. 379-81.
42/ Peratis and Ross, "Primer," p. 75.
43/ Ibid.
44/ Ibid., p. 76.

Index of Persons and Subjects

Index of Scripture References